THE INNER GAME OF TRADING

Creating the Winner's State of Mind

**ROBERT KOPPEL
AND HOWARD ABELL**

McGraw-Hill

New York   San Francisco   Washington, D.C.   Auckland   Bogotá
Caracas   Lisbon   London   Madrid   Mexico City   Milan
Montreal   New Delhi   San Juan   Singapore
Sydney   Tokyo   Toronto

McGraw-Hill

A Division of The McGraw·Hill Companies

1 2 3 4 5 6 7 8 9 0 BB 9 0 2 1 0 9 8 7

ISBN 0-7863-1189-4

Printed and bound by Braun Brumfield

This publication is designed to provide accurate and authoritative information in regard to the subject matter covered. It is sold with the understanding that neither the author nor the publisher is engaged in rendering legal, accounting, or other professional service. If legal advice or other expert assistance is required, the services of a competent professional person should be sought.

> *—From a Declaration of Principles jointly adopted by a Committee of the American Bar Association and a Committee of Publishers.*

McGraw-Hill books are available at special quantity discounts to use as premiums and sales promotions, or for use in corporate training programs. For more information, please write to the Director of Special Sales, McGraw-Hill, 11 West 19th Street, New York, NY 10011. Or contact your local bookstore.

To Our Families

Mara, Lily and Niko

Roslyn and Alex

"We must not be misled to our own detriment to assume that the horseless carriage can displace the proved and tried horse."
— John K. Herr (1878-1955)
Major General, U.S. Army

"As far as sinking a ship with a bomb is concerned, it just can't be done."
— Clark Woodward (1877-1967)
Rear Admiral, U.S. Navy

"That is the biggest fool thing we have ever done . . . The atomic bomb will never go off, and I speak as an expert in explosives."
— William Leahy (1875-1959)
Admiral, U.S. Navy

"Rail travel at high speeds is not possible because passengers, unable to breathe, will die of asphyxia."
— Dionysius Lardner (1793-1859)
English Scientist

"Radio has no future."

— William Thomson
President of the Royal Society of Science

"While theoretically and technically television may be feasible, commercially and financially I consider it an impossibility."
— Lee Deforest (1873-1961)
American Inventor

"Man Is What He Believes."

— Anton Chekhov

Contents

Preface   ix

Acknowledgments   xiii

I   **THE INNERGAME**   1

1   On the Nature of Becoming a Successful Trader   13

2   The Power of Belief and Focus   19

3   Goal Setting and Motivation   21

4   The Edge That Makes the Difference   31

II   **THE MODELING OF EXCELLENCE**   35

5   The Syntax of Successful Trading   37

6   Winning States of Mind   41

7   Matching a Trading Style to Your Personality   63

CONTENTS

III THE TOP TRADERS:
**Successful Trading Demonstrated
through the Prism of Real Traders** 67

8 Motive and Motivation 73

9 Successful Trading 77

10 Words of Advice 85

11 Leo Melamed 87

12 John F. (Jack) Sandner 107

13 Jeffrey L. Silverman 127

14 Bruce Johnson 145

IV THE PSYCHOLOGY OF TECHNICAL
ANALYSIS:
A Random Walk Down a Crowded Lane 157

15 Trends and the Efficient Market Theory 161

16 Money Management 169

17 Classical Chart Analysis 171

V WINNING VERSUS LOSING 189

18 Principles of Successful Trading 191

19 Characteristics of Winning 195

Index 203

Preface

"'Begin at the beginning,' the King said gravely, 'and go 'til you come to the end; then stop.'"

—Lewis Carroll, *Alice's Adventures in Wonderland*

There is a story we once heard a psychology professor tell of a woman who consulted a family counselor regarding her marital problems. "Do you have grounds?" asked the therapist. "Yes," replied the woman, "Two and a half acres." "No," he replied, "I mean, do you have a grudge?" "A grudge?" answered the woman. "No, but we have a carport." Growing more frustrated the counselor shot back, "Does he beat you up?"

"Beat me up?" came the response, "Hell no! I'm up an hour earlier than that old dog every morning!"

"Mrs. Brown!!" exclaimed the counselor, "You are seeking help from me because of a problem you are having with your husband. For God's sake what is his problem?"

The woman hesitated for a moment and then unloaded, "The man just doesn't know how to communicate!"

What does this story have to do with trading futures? . . . Everything! Over 80 percent of all futures traders are net losers and it is our unqualified belief, based on 40 years of combined experience in this industry as exchange members (clearing and trading), traders, personal trainers, and consultants, that the reason such a staggering number of people lose year in and year out is because they don't know how to communicate—with themselves. To succeed at trading, like anything else, requires enormous discipline: to establish a goal, to adopt a personal course of action, and finally to take action on a consistent basis, making the necessary adjustments and refinements as conditions and experience deem appropriate.

It is effective action that produces results which ultimately assures success. Ironically, we live in an age of information, but information alone is not enough; how we communicate with ourselves determines how much of what we know we will use as traders and as human beings.

There are more titles available today on trading futures than ever before, from the very general to the highly rarefied. In recent years, several books have also been published on the psychology of trading, and although some of them offer useful information and insights of a general or conversational nature, none to our knowledge have been written by professional traders who have experienced the blood, sweat, and tears of their subject, and who possess a formal understanding of the inner psychology of trading. Specifically, we know of no work based on the ongoing rough and tumble of day-to-day trading, focusing on the specific internal elements within all of us that form the basis for how we communicate with ourselves: the ways and things we visualize, hear, and feel, which in gross terms determine the difference between being a winner or a loser.

The great single truth behind successful trading is this: successful traders produce exactly the results they want through specific physical and mental actions. It's important to bear in mind the opposite is true as well. Losses too, are the result of individual production; that is, we don't just catch them as if we were contracting the common cold.

Through the prism of professionally recognized top traders, we get a unique glimpse of the internal terrain of consistent winners, how they overcome the barriers and frustrations that hold most people back. What keeps them going is not a love affair with risk taking, as you might think. These are not the daredevils of futures trading, but what they do possess is the ability to keep moving forward undeterred by setbacks.

Finally, and most importantly, the kind of effective personal communication and internal discipline that characterize successful trading can be learned like any skill; however, it requires daily conditioning. You wouldn't work out just once and conclude that you're physically fit. Similarly with trading—it's an ongoing, life-long process.

W.D. Gann, arguably one of the greatest traders who ever lived, summed it up when he wrote, "I have studied and improved my methods every year for the past forty years. I am still learning. I hope to make greater discoveries in the future."

We opened with a quote from Lewis Carroll; we would like to offer a short addendum. There is no end in sight!

Successful Trading!

Bob Koppel

Howard Abell

Acknowledgments

Many thanks go to the traders who graciously agreed to be interviewed for *The Innergame of Trading*. Despite demanding schedules, each was forthcoming and generously accommodating. We deeply appreciate their candor and insights into how their minds work.

We would like to thank Mara Koppel for reading the original manuscript and for providing fine editing suggestions. Bob feels fortunate to have a wife who is not only a good friend but who can write a good sentence. He wishes also to thank his children, Lily and Niko; their analytical minds, humor, and understanding have given him a much deeper appreciation of the innergame of fatherhood.

Howard would like to thank Roslyn Kolin Abell, a loving friend, for her encouragement and intellectual support during the writing of this book. Her trading experience and insights proved invaluable. Mention must also be made of Alex Abell's readings of the early drafts. His comments and suggestions were most helpful. Thanks also go to our editors, Janet St. John and Kevin Thornton, for their deep insights into making the final manuscript live up to our high expectations.

Finally, we would like to thank Kevin Commins and the staff at Probus Publishing for a wealth of ideas and uncompromising support throughout this project. Marshall McLuhan is reported to have said, "Gutenberg made everybody a reader; Xerox makes everybody a publisher." Kevin is a rare publisher indeed.

PART I

THE INNERGAME

In the mid-1920s, by most accounts, John D. Rockefeller was the richest man in the world. Whatever he lay his hands on turned almost instantly to gold: stocks, bonds, oil wells; the man truly possessed the Midas Touch. A *New York Times* reporter intrigued by Rockefeller's financial genius prodded him to reveal his formula for monetary success.

"To what do you owe your astonishing success?" asked the reporter.

"Simple," answered Rockefeller, "I owe all my wealth to three things that if carefully followed anyone can achieve unimaginable riches. First, I arrived at work earlier and with more energy and enthusiasm than any of my co-workers. Second, I departed from work later and with a greater sense of accomplishment. And third, I struck oil!"

Unfortunately, the authors of this book can not help you strike oil; however, we can point you to a fathomless "oil well" that has the potential to pay off big in the futures market—you! It is our intention to assist you in the development of this natural resource and to help you tap it. The natural resource to which we refer is your internal psychological landscape which determines your level of confidence, self-esteem, personal beliefs, focus, and state of mind; all of which will predict ultimate success or failure in the futures market. Learning how to control this resource in order to achieve positive trading results is what we call the innergame of trading.

It has been our observation that most books on trading read either like military manuals, compliance forms from a regulatory agency, or instruction booklets from a Tokyo watchmaker about how to set the third time zone function on your digital wristwatch, translated from Japanese into Czechoslovakian, then to Swahili, and at last into English. Our intention therefore is to make this book first and foremost eminently readable and second, a useful and well-used handbook. We encourage you to write in its margin and underline freely—let the pages become dog-eared! In short, our objective is to assist you in helping yourself to become a more successful trader. As we begin we would like to say that all that follows is based on certain assumptions that we have learned over many years, and experienced, at times painfully, as professional traders. The validity of these assumptions have also been confirmed in our interviews with some of the very best traders in the futures industry. They are:

- Commodity prices are not random. There is an underlying order to all markets and price action.
- Great trading can be taught. It is a skill that can be learned; which is to say, one need not be born with a constitutional or genetic propensity to become the Michael Jordan of the futures market.
- People can and do consistently make money in the futures market utilizing a wide variety of successful strategies and techniques.
- Your state of mind, focus, and personal belief system will be the determining factors for your success as a trader, *not* your trading system.
- Discipline produces confidence.
- You must understand and act on your motives and goals for trading.

Having stated our assumptions about trading, we must ask you, the reader, the overriding question, why do *you* want to trade?

Ask a crowded room of traders why they trade and you will get as many responses as there are traders. Yes, making money is a very important reason, but if it is your only reason for trading you are setting yourself up for inevitable disappointment. As Joel Greenberg put it, "I love the excitement of fitting the pieces into the jigsaw puzzle of trading—the money is great but it's the intellectual challenge that keeps me going." Very few successful traders, in our experience, just focus on the money; in fact, the money is almost always the end product of some greater internal reason to trade. "I love wrastling with the alligators. If at the end of a day I get to dance at the ball, that's O.K. but it's the day-to-day combat that juices me, that keeps me coming back for more," is the way another top trader put it.

It is essential that you understand your motive for trading. So we must therefore begin by asking *you* why do you want to trade? Now don't just answer matter of factly. Write down why specifically you have chosen to trade. What is it that attracts you to trading? Use the following space to detail your answer.

_____

_____

_____

_____

_____

As you analyze the motives for trading that you have written down, is it essential for you to trade in order to satisfy this motive? For example, if your motive is excitement, can you satisfy this need by sky-diving or windsurfing? If the answer is yes, stop reading here! Do not go any farther! If you hadn't already written on this page, we would suggest you return *The Innergame of Trading* for its full price; however, considering the book's current condition you might want to trade it in at a used bookstore. On the other hand, you may want to pass it on to a friend or colleague who has a burning, insatiable appetite to become a successful trader and who wants to learn as much as possible about himself and the futures market.

Now that you are aware of your core motives for trading, the whys so to speak, behind all your trading actions, how does possessing this knowledge place you on the road to becoming a more successful trader? The answer should appear obvious. Your motives will dictate the intent and intensity of any course of action that you adopt in the market. The whys produce the hows. For example, if your core motive for trading is the intrinsic intellectual challenge of beating the market, then choosing a personal trading style and strategy that consciously builds into it the awareness of this motive will help determine your market behavior.

Motive will dictate how and on what you focus, the level of confidence and esteem you experience, the efficacy or limitation of personal beliefs (as they relate to trading), and the degree to which your state of mind is positive and resourceful. In short, all the necessary ingredients for successful trading.

Figure I-1—The Importance of Motive to Successful Trading

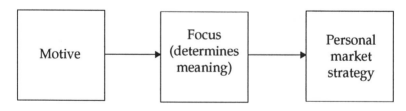

"To motivate yourself, identify your motives and take action on them!"

— Zig Ziglar

If you turn to almost any book on trading you will see some or all of the following trading rules.

Figure I-2—Trading Axioms

- ☐ Manage your money well.
- ☐ Don't overtrade
- ☐ Don't turn a profit into a loss.
- ☐ The trend is your friend.
- ☐ Learn how to use orders properly.
- ☐ Don't add to a loser.
- ☐ Take big profits.
- ☐ Take small losses.
- ☐ Don't get stubborn.
- ☐ Buy low, sell high.
- ☐ Avoid the crowd.
- ☐ Buy the rumor, sell the facts.
- ☐ The market is always right.
- ☐ Avoid fear and greed.
- ☐ Trade liquid markets.
- ☐ Don't buy or sell on price alone.
- ☐ Preserve capital.

There are others of course and almost everyone knows these market axioms, but the question remains, why are there so few top traders? The answer has less to do with objective rules and systems and more to do with subjective experience: how we see, hear, and "feel" markets, and then relate that information to ourselves before we move to action, that is, before we make a trade.

Historically, books on trading have assumed psychological skills are innate, that traders either possess them or they don't. To use the vernacular, it is assumed one either has mental toughness or nerve, or it is believed that one lacks the disposition necessary to trade; however, like trading itself, psychological skills need to be identified, learned, and practiced.

Figure I-3—The Psychological Skills Necessary to Become a Successful Trader

- Compelling personal motivation.
- Goal setting.
- Confidence.
- Anxiety control.
- Focus.
- State management.
- Positive and empowering self-talk.
- Mental conditioning.

As we review the skills mentioned in Figure I-3, we must ask ourselves two basic questions: (1) What are the market behaviors which prevent most traders from achieving the results they desire? (2) What psychological factors inhibit most traders from applying specific skills when trading?

In our experience and in the view of the top traders we have interviewed, the following are the essential psychological barriers to successful trading.

Figure I-4—The Essential Psychological Barriers to Successful Trading

- Not defining a loss.

- Not taking a loss or a profit.
- Getting locked into a belief.
- Getting "Boston-Strangled."
- Kamikaze trading.
- Euphoric trading.
- Hesitating at your numbers.
- Not catching a breakout.
- Not focusing on opportunities.
- Being more invested in being right than in making money.
- Not consistently applying your trading system.
- Not having a well-defined money management program.
- Not being in the right state of mind.

1. Not Defining a Loss

No one enters a trade assuming it will result in a loss. No one buys expecting the market has topped out; conversely, no one sells expecting the market to rally to new highs. However, this occurs all too often. So upon entering any market, it is important that you have your downside defined, not after you enter a trade but before! If you are afraid to take a loss, don't trade.

2. Not Taking a Loss or a Profit

There is an old trading axiom "your first loss is the best loss." It's true. Losing is an integral part of the process. So is the opposite, taking profits. If the market has reached your objective, don't be afraid to ring the register. Many times the market will not give you a second chance.

3. Getting Locked into a Belief

That is exactly what it is—prison. As George Segal succinctly put it, "The market is the boss." Your belief that silver is going to the moon or the dollar is going to hell in a handbasket is irrelevant. The market tells you everything! Listen! Remember what Yogi Berra said, "You can observe a lot by just watching."

4. Getting "Boston Strangled"

There is an old Henny Youngman joke that was popular in the early 1960s at the time the Boston strangler was not yet in police custody. A man is sitting in his living room, reading the evening newspaper and he hears a knock at the front door. Walking up to the door but not opening it he asks, "Who is it?"

The psychopath answers, "It's the Boston strangler."

The man walks back into the apartment, passes the living room and into the kitchen, turns to his wife and says, "It's for you, dear!"

We always relate this anecdote at our seminars as an analogy to taking a trade that you have no control over, from someone else. In other words, a tip is like getting Boston strangled. Don't do it! This is one door you don't want to open!

5. Kamikaze Trading

Trading like you're a kamikaze pilot on his 44th mission. Perhaps you're feeling betrayed, angry; you need revenge. Snap out of it! You're going to crash land.

6. Euphoric Trading

The opposite of kamikaze trading. You're feeling absolutely invincible. Heroic. Untouchable. Look out!

7. Hesitating at Your Numbers

You've done all this work—daily, weekly, and monthly charts. You've studied Gann, Fibonnaci, Wycoff, and Elliott Wave. The market comes right down to your number, line, area, but *you* can't buy it!

8. Not Catching a Breakout

It's like going to the airport and watching the planes take off. Wouldn't it be fun just once to be on board and arrive at an exciting destination!

9. Not Focusing on Opportunities

There are so many distractions in the market. How do you keep your focus clear, laser-straight? How do you get beyond all the head fakes?

10. Being More Invested in Being Right Than in Making Money

In almost every trading room throughout the world, there are people who run around announcing to their colleagues that they have the high/low of every move in almost every market. What they don't possess are profits. The name of the game is making money. And yes, it's only a game!

11. Not Consistently Applying Your Trading System

If it's any good, you have to use it consistently. As the saying goes, "If you don't use it . . . lose it."

12. Not Having a Well-Defined Money Management Program

You have heard this one many times before, "But the trade looked so good, so right." The object of money management is preservation of capital.

13. Not Being in the Right State of Mind

In our experience, over 80 percent of all trading failure is the result of not being in the right state of mind. The right state of mind produces the right results. As Gene Agatstein observed, "You get exactly the results you want. You produce your own success."

Successful trading then, in essence, comes down to this: overcoming your personal psychological barriers and conditioning yourself to produce feelings of self-trust, high self-esteem, unshakable conviction, and confidence which will naturally lead to good judgment and winning trades based on a proven methodology. But how do you do it? Patience.

Chapter One

On the Nature of Becoming a Successful Trader

![separator]

The Four Cs

Have you ever wanted to make an important change in your life but failed? Have you ever tried to kick a really bad habit but could not follow through? Have you ever had the desire to become really successful at something but lacked the conviction? If so, welcome to the human race. We can all answer affirmatively, in different degrees, to any or all of these questions. But how does this relate to trading? It relates to trading in this way: If you choose to become a successful trader, it is like undertaking any important change, and in order to succeed specific conditions must be met. The characteristics of successful trading are:

- Know your outcome.
- Develop a plan of action.
- Reevaluate and retool.

1. Know Your Outcome

You must have an end point in mind. It is important that you know exactly, in detail, what you want to accomplish in quantifiable and verifiable terms. "I want to become a successful trader and for me this means . . . and I know I'm successful when . . ."

2. Develop a Plan of Action

You must develop a program, a personal strategy to accomplish this end, based on homework, hard work, and discipline.

3. Reevaluate and Retool

Successful trading like success itself is not a single mountain to be climbed or a static "thing" to be possessed. If you want to succeed at trading, it must be viewed as a process, a continuously changing dialogue of the mind fraught with peril but offering great rewards. So you must be able to adjust to changing conditions. When things work, use them; when they don't, discard them and move on. There are untold riches to be gained in the futures markets but you need the sensory acuity to be able to discern between winning and losing strategies, and to act accordingly. Have you ever observed a toddler who is in the process of learning to walk? The child employs a host of strategies before he or she is successful. You must view success at trading with the same perspective of flexibility and persistence.

What All Traders Share in Common

All traders, from the novice to the most highly successful, have these things in common: They lose, get frustrated, at times feel lousy, and experience stress and disappointment. But the top traders, at varying points in their careers, undertook to develop personal strategies for overcoming these types of setbacks. They taught themselves specific, however varying, methods for getting around potentially disabling psychological bends in the road, techniques and strategies that you can learn too.

Wanting to become a winning trader in psychological terms is not very different from choosing to make any significant improvement in your life (e.g., getting in shape). It requires a four-part process which we call The Four Cs of Top Trading:

- Commitment
- Conviction
- Constructing new patterns of behavior
- Conditioning

1. Commitment

All significant change begins with a strong overriding motive to succeed. Picture the intensity of Larry Bird, Pete Rose or Magic Johnson. Top performing traders have a commitment to overcome any hardship or setback to achieve their goals. They are also not afraid to play the game.

There is a wonderful anecdote about a poor overworked guy who goes to church and prays.

"Please, Lord," he incants, "Let me win the lottery."

A week goes by and nothing happens. That Sunday, the man returns to church and once again prays, "Dear Lord would it really hurt you if I won the lottery?" Still there is no winning number.

Six months pass and the man, determined to win the lottery and having great faith in the power of prayer, returns to church and in his most impassioned, supplicating voice, looking heavenward begins, "Oh, Lord. If only you could let me win this week's lottery."

Suddenly he is interrupted in mid-prayer by a divine voice that emanates from the church rafters.

"John," begins the voice, "You've gotta buy a ticket!"

It's the same thing with trading. If you want to succeed, you have to buy a ticket. Commitment is your entrance pass.

2. Conviction

Have you ever observed young children trying to drive their parent's car? They bounce up and down, to and fro in front of the steering wheel. In their minds, they believe their movements will dictate the movement of the car; but the car stands still because it needs a key to turn on the ignition. When it comes to operating in the marketplace, developing a system of beliefs that fosters excellence is the ignition necessary to fire up the engine of great trading. It is critical for you to possess a range of positive beliefs about yourself and success in the market in order to achieve optimum results. As Bruce Johnson put it, "You gotta believe the markets exist just so you can make money."

3. Constructing New Patterns of Behavior

If you want to lose weight, you have to stop eating french fried potatoes and drinking ice cream sodas. There's no way around it! You must interrupt old patterns of behavior and substitute them with new ones. If you have trouble taking losses in the market or buying when everyone else is selling, or catching breakouts, guess what you have to do to become more successful! Top traders have developed techniques for constructing new patterns of behavior that empower them to act decisively and automatically. So can you!

4. Conditioning

Finally, once a new pattern of winning behavior has been sub-
stituted for a losing one, it is not enough to apply this new
approach just once. You must condition yourself—to buy
breaks/sell rallies/buy your numbers—to trade your system. In
short, you must discipline yourself, literally *condition* your nervous system to act automatically and unemotionally. Discipline
does and will produce confidence and ultimate success.

Chapter Two

The Power of Belief and Focus

Belief is the window through which we see the world and through which we see ourselves. Whatever you do in life will be affected by what you believe in; that is to say, what you believe about yourself and others. Your actions are a direct result of the quality and intensity of your beliefs. What does this have to do with trading? Well, trading is an expression of human action, isn't it?

Let's take a look at a situation which has nothing at all to do with trading. Picture yourself in a conference room with twenty people, one of whom is from the planet Venus. Yes, we know this is highly unlikely but let's pretend. Let's also pretend that you have an abiding belief in the inferiority of Venutians; you believe they are lazy, foul-smelling, and shiftless creatures. When someone suggests you select as a partner the person next to you, who happens to be a Venutian, you are a) overjoyed at the prospect of having the honor to work with a creature from another planet, b) indifferent, c) angry as hell that you're stuck with a stinking Venutian.

I think you will agree, the answer is obvious. Now let's consider a similar situation with one slight revision. Picture yourself in that same conference room. Let's pretend you respect the intelligence and enterprise of Venutians. You believe in their superior capacities of mind and behavior. I think you will agree that now you do not feel angry or stuck with a Venutian as a partner. In fact, you feel quite the opposite.

Likewise, what you believe about yourself as a trader will determine not only the results of your trading decisions but also how you experience the entire trading process. A belief is nothing more than a deeply felt certainty which we possess about ourselves and the world we live in. What we believe, literally what we feel, determines what we focus on; what meaning we assign to what we see and what actions result. This process of belief → focus → action not only determines our success as traders but in a very real sense, our success as human beings.

Figure 2-1—The Power of Belief and Focus in Making Successful Trading Decisions

Positive Trading Belief System	→ Focus → (Dictated by Belief)	Trading Decision (Directed by Focus)
"I'm a disciplined trader." "I can make money by capitalizing on opportunities."	"I buy at my chart point according to a specific game plan with a defined loss."	"I confidently take a profit or loss based on a well-planned methodology."

Chapter Three

Goal Setting and Motivation

We live in a world where anything is possible, where one's belief determines focus and that focus becomes reality. Think of Whitney Houston, Michael Jordan, Ervin Johnson, Gloria Estafan, and Bill Clinton. Consider what all these individuals have in common. Of course they possess great ability in their chosen profession, but they also have a personal strategy, a plan, a road map of success if you will, that allows them to identify and achieve their goals.

If you were planning a trip from New York to California wouldn't you have a map to chart your ultimate destination? Then why is it that most traders, certainly the less successful ones, lack a clearly defined set of trading goals?

It reminds us of the following story.

Two lumberjacks were cutting trees deep in the north woods. After several hours of sawing, one of the lumberjacks noticed his partner was hardly a sixteenth of an inch into the tree.

"Hey, Bob," he remarked, "You're not making any progress."

"I know, I know," he repeated, "Don't bother me."

"But Bob," continued the first lumberjack, "You've got to stop and sharpen your blade."

"Stop? I can't stop," he answered pointing to his poor performance, "I've got to cut down this tree!"

That's how it is with most traders; they're too busy sawing. They don't take the time to sharpen their blades, to clearly define their trading goals.

Figure 3-1—The Importance of Trading Goals

Goal	Benefit	Trading Behavior
Performance goal	Focuses on improvement in relation to your own standards.	Increases physical and psychological skills related to trading.
Outcome goal	Helps determine what's important to you.	Allows for the development of techniques and strategies which match your personality.
Motivation goal	Helps increase effort, direct attention.	Allows traders to maintain a high level of enthusiasm and confidence.

When we do personal training with individual traders we always begin by having them answer the following questions:

- Do I have in writing a clearly defined set of trading goals?
- Do I have a similar set of goals for the next six weeks, six months, six years?

- Have I specifically done something today to move me closer to my short-term goal? My long-term goals?
- Do I have a clear idea of what I want to accomplish with my trading today, this week?
- Do I concentrate on goals rather than procedures?
- Do I evaluate my progress based on accomplishment rather than activity?

Establishing goals not only identifies exactly what we want to accomplish as traders; it also serves to motivate us. There has been ample research which demonstrates the importance of a clearly defined goal as a compelling source of positive personal motivation.

So what are trading goals? The criteria for a trading goal should satisfy the basic requirements of any goal. The mnemonic we choose to use is SToP CRiMe. A goal should be the following:

Figure 3-2—Operational Definition of Trading Goals

Specific—clear, precise, well defined.

Time-framed—state within a specific time period.

Positive—state it in a way that is empowering.

Control—it should be completely within your control.

Realistic—making a million on your first trade does not satisfy our definition.

Measurable—easily quantifiable.

We would now like to direct your attention to *your* specific trading goals. We encourage you to spend time on these goals—don't just keep sawing away. Take the time to sharpen your blade by answering these questions. The more you put into this exercise, the greater the return. Research has found that writing down your goals greatly increases your commitment and the likelihood of achieving your goals. So, let's begin.

1. What are your trading goals? What do you want to accomplish? What is your long-term goal?

_____

_____

_____

_____

2. Why is it important for you to achieve these goals?

_____

_____

_____

_____

3. What is preventing you from achieving your goals right now? Be honest with yourself!

_____

_____

_____

_____

4. What specific action or steps can you take to achieve your goals today and in the future?

_____

_____

_____

_____

Now that you have answered these questions and have a better understanding of your personal goals, let's take a look at the goals of others. The following are a list of trading goals from traders we have worked with on an individual basis and from participants in our trading seminars. As you consider these goals, be reminded that individuals were asked to have these goals satisfy all the criteria of goal setting that we discussed earlier. In other words, operational definitions were required when individuals stated abstract ideas.

- To have more control over my emotions when I trade.
- To have more confidence when taking losses.
- To be consistently profitable.
- To develop a system that is consistent with my personality and to readily apply it.
- To define my losses and not dwell on them.
- To consistently be aware that trading is a process and not just a series of independent trades.
- To have a high level of self-esteem when I trade.
- To be a disciplined trader.
- To focus on opportunities.
- To catch breakouts.
- To take all my signals.
- To have control over my trades.
- To establish limited risk and limitless profit potential.

- To become a better trader by constantly trying to learn more—about myself.
- To operate completely in the here and now.

Figure 3-3—Monthly Goal Chart

- My long-term goal is _____
- My goal for this month is _____
- My goal for this week is _____
- My strategy for achieving this goal is _____

  _____

  _____

  _____

  _____

As you think about what you have written, we want you to become aware of those factors or personal anxieties which you have identified as impediments to achieving your goals.

We believe, based on our experience and interviews, that the factors which have prevented most traders from achieving their trading goals fall into five broad categories. They are:

Figure 3-4—The Factors Which Prevent Traders from Achieving Their Trading Goals

- Self-limiting beliefs.
- Unresourceful state.
- Poor focus.
- Ill-defined personal strategy.
- Lack of physical and psychological energy.

1. Self-Limiting Beliefs

Self-limiting beliefs are inhibiting beliefs that traders possess about themselves and/or the market. Examples of such beliefs are:

"I don't have enough conviction."

"I'm never quite sure I know what I'm doing."

"How can I be sure?"

"I can't trust my judgment."

"I don't believe in myself."

"It's impossible to make money in these markets."

2. Unresourceful State

An unresourceful state is when a trader is in a state of mind that is guided by fear, anxiety, and confusion. Traders reported the following.

"I'm really angry."

"God, is this frustrating."

"I'm too stupid."

"I'm afraid."

"I'm too small a player."

3. Poor Focus

Poor focus is when trades are made as a result of distracted concentration. You can't zero in on the essentials. Traders have said:

"Those bad fills always get in my way."

"I'm always thinking about something else at just the wrong time."

"I'm so distracted by procedures I don't have time to look at what's really important."

"I can't see the big picture."

4. Ill-Defined Personal Strategy

An ill-defined personal strategy is characterized by trades that are made by the seat of one's pants. In this condition, trading is nothing more than an immediate response to emotion. Traders who have experienced this report:

"I don't have a clear plan."

"I never know when to take profits."

"My methodology lacks consistency."

"Sometimes it works and sometimes it doesn't."

"How do you know when to get out of a market?"

5. Lack of Physical and Psychological Energy

Lack of physical and psychological energy occurs when one's anxiety level produces tension which results in physical and phychological fatigue. Traders have told us:

"These markets totally wipe me out."

"I just don't have enough energy."

"The market action just drives me nuts."

Figure 3-5—Sources of Trading Anxiety

Anxiety	Manifestation of Trading Behavior
Fear of Failure	Trader feels intense pressure to perform, ties self-worth to trading, perfectionist. Trader is concerned about what others think.

Anxiety	*Manifestation of Trading Behavior*
Fear of Success	Trader loses control, euphoric trading. Trader doubts himself.
Fear of Inadequacy	Trader experiences loss of self-esteem, diminished confidence.
Loss of Control	Trader loses sense of personal responsibility when trading. Trader feels market is out to get him.

The prescription we would like to offer to overcome these psychological roadblocks is what we call the edge that makes the difference.

Chapter Four

The Edge That Makes the Difference

Traders always speak of "getting the edge" and this is particularly true of the most successful traders. However, without exception, the top traders understand that the edge has little to do with the commonsense or conventional notion of getting a good fill in the market or being stopped out exactly at your price. And it makes little difference if these traders employ fundamental or technical analysis, whether they are day traders or position themselves for the long pull. The idea that was repeated time and time again by the top traders was that an edge is essential, and their edge is the overriding ability to be resilient to whatever the market sends in their direction: weathering difficult times, even "busting out" with little emotional impact, being able to maintain unassailable confidence in themselves at all times. For these top performers, trading is a game and although methodologies vary widely, they all shared in common a burning, unquenchable desire to become successful at trading (however they define success), often at significant personal and professional expense. Other commonalities in capturing the edge included:

- A personal discipline based on hard work, independence, and patience.
- A love of trading.

- Well-defined risk management.
- Total acceptance of losing as part of the trading process.

Figure 4-1—Critical Factors in Determining the Edge That Makes the Difference

Trader Response	*Having the Edge*	*Losing the Edge*
Patience	Waits for opportunities to materialize based on well thought out game plan.	Little planning; reacts according to personal whim.
Discipline	Sees the big picture, responds deliberately.	Emotional, anxious; often confused about what to do.
Strategy	Highly planned; limits losses, lets profits run.	Little planning, does not rely on consistent methodology.
Expertise	Well prepared—has done the necessary homework.	Little market knowledge; unprepared.
Motive	Long-term motive, e.g., intellectual challenge.	To make money, instant gratification.
Goals	Clearly defined.	Ill-defined.
Risk Control	Highly controlled risk/reward ratio.	Little or no control over risk/reward ratio.

Trader Response	Having the Edge	Losing the Edge
State of Mind	Positive, resourceful, empowering beliefs and focus. High level of self-esteem and trust; relaxed and confident.	Nervous, anxious, believes the worst will happen. Focus is distracted. Trades in conflict.

The edge that makes the difference then comes down to this:

1. Fully Understand Your Motive for Trading

Once you know what your motives are, examine them carefully. Most traders trade in a constant state of conflict. It has been our experience that many people who think they want to trade really don't. In addition, your motive should include a strong need for personal independence which is crucial.

2. Develop a Personal Strategy That Works for You and Fits Your Personality

If the system doesn't feel right, you're going to lose before you even start.

3. It Has to Be Fun

We can't stress this point enough. Trading has to literally feel good. Which is to say, you must be in a frame of mind which allows you to enjoy the process effortlessly, be resourceful, and make good judgments.

4. Hard Work Is Essential

There's no way to get around it. You must put in the time. As Woody Allen said, "Ninety percent of existence is showing up." You must also be able to keep trading in perspective.

5. Confidence

You must possess a repertoire of personal beliefs that constantly reinforces feelings of high self-esteem and confidence in your analysis and execution of trades, whether you win or lose. Needless to say, discipline, patience, personal responsibility, and repeated success make this a lot easier.

6. Positive State of Mind

If there is a single variable which guarantees success, it is this one. The top-performing traders have developed an internal terrain that reduces anxiety and promotes excellence. They manage to achieve this end by internally representing external events in such a way that assures success, adjusting and redefining as they deem appropriate. They do this by employing a belief system that does not allow for the concept of failure and a personal focus which concentrates on what is essential to achieving this end. In short, they have mastered the ability to create states of mind and body that are resourceful and assure whatever it takes to succeed. Exactly how they do this we will show you in the next chapter.

PART II

THE MODELING OF EXCELLENCE

Chapter Five

The Syntax of Successful Trading

In its conventional sense, syntax refers to the arrangement of words or phrases in a sentence. In the sentence, "Tom eats chicken," the meaning is quite clear; however, the meaning is very different from a sentence which employs the same words but in a different syntactical order as in "Chicken eats Tom." In each of these sentences the experience is different for both the bird and for Tom. The arrangement, or syntax in which external stimuli are first presented and then internally represented to our brain, will determine our specific and resulting behavior. Representing external events in the "right order" will produce the result we desire.

By now you're wondering, once again, what on earth does this have to do with trading? Have you ever had the experience in the market that you were long and hoped and prayed that the market would go up . . . but it didn't? It just sat there, or worse yet, it went lower and lower and just at the instant you abandoned the trade, it did exactly what you had originally anticipated and went skyrocketing toward new highs. We've all experienced this situation and some of us at considerable expense. In fact, most of us have experienced this sort of thing more than once and, dare I say, even routinely, almost to the point of habit; so, that when the money is being made by others you feel like you're on the sidelines watching someone else run down field for the winning touchdown.

What we learn from the top traders is that successful trading has its own syntax; its own arrangement of internal representations and concomitant, proven market behaviors that are executed in a specific sequence of actions to achieve a profitable result. In contrast, the way most traders internally represent market phenomena dictates a response of indecision, anxiety, or confusion and produces a result which they find ungratifying. The important point here is that we always produce the exact result that is true to our syntax (our strategy).

Ideally the syntax of successful trading looks like this:

Figure 5-1—The Trading Syntax of the Successful Trader

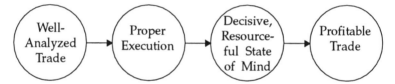

The trading syntax of the successful trader is a specific strategy for producing a particular result, namely, making a profit. In a way, it is similar to following a recipe. If you cook with the same ingredients, given similar conditions, you will repeatedly come up with the same result. If you follow the recipe of top traders, that is to say, if you model their internal representations, strategies, beliefs, and behaviors, you will produce the same successful outcomes.

What would it mean to be able to routinely produce the strategy of the industry's top traders? How important would it be to understand how great traders deal with internal and external stimuli? How would it make a difference to your trading to know their personal syntax for representing the external chaos of market action and then converting that information into a well-organized internal strategy for competent and automatic action? The answer is obvious and you will soon know how they do it.

Chapter Six

Winning States of Mind

The difference between winning and losing, success and failure, depends on just a few simple but profound choices. Ironically, knowledge alone will not provide the solution. It is not enough to know what to do. You must consistently do what you know. It is not sufficient to know what the top traders do. That is, in order to model them you must adopt the same or similar trading actions based on similar beliefs, focuses, and states of mind. In short, we must employ their positive, resourceful, internal states to produce external excellence.

Figure 6-1: The Winning State of Mind

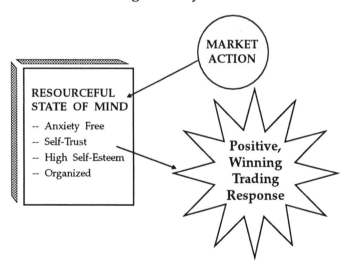

In order to describe the syntax of the winning state of mind, we would like to begin by posing a question. Have you ever felt really inept at something? Whatever you did or tried to do just went wrong; you felt as though you were just a living example of Murphy's law—whatever can go wrong does go wrong. We know we've had days like that and quite a few involved trading.

Now we would like to ask you another question. Have you ever had the opposite experience? Where you felt absolutely confident; whatever you touched seemed to turn to gold. You were just riding so high you might have thought to yourself "Damn, I'm good." We personally remember a trader who we had known for many years as a near-reclusive, withdrawn individual skipping around the S and P pit chirping those exact words the day of the October 1987 Stock Market crash when he was short.

But to get back to our subject, why is it that sometimes you feel and act so inept and other times so competent? Why is it that sometimes you're riding high in the saddle and other times you're staring that horse right in the butt. We suggest it has all to do with your state of mind.

Your state of mind then is how you are feeling at any given moment in time, how you are relating to the world. As we have stated above, your state of mind determines your capability and is not in any way a reflection of your ultimate ability, which is why at times you feel or act as if you are inept in the market even though you're not. After all, you have made a winning trade at least once, haven't you?

If you change your state of mind from negative to positive you increase your level of resourcefulness; you allow yourself to move from a psychological position of reduced capacity to optimum personal achievement. Aha, now you finally see how all this relates to trading! Just think what it would mean to always trade in a positive, resourceful, fully organized state of mind.

In our seminars, we always ask the participants to answer the following questions. Please take the time to answer each question in as detailed and thoughtful a way as possible. Once again, the more you put into this exercise the better the result.

1. How much money have you lost in the past few years trading because you hadn't managed your state of mind?

_____

_____

_____

_____

_____

2. What has been the emotional cost of not having traded in the right state of mind?

_____

_____

_____

_____

_____

3. How much more money would you make if you always traded in a positive, resourceful state of mind?

_____

_____

_____

_____

4. How much more fun would you have if you consistently managed your state of mind? (Yes, it is possible.)

_____

_____

_____

_____

_____

5. How would the entire quality of your life be enhanced if you were in a peak state of mind every day?

_____

_____

_____

_____

_____

Fully understanding your state of mind is the key to adopting competent strategies for change and, ultimately, to achieving consistently successful trading results.

Complete the following exercise by rating your internal state on a scale of 1-5. Of course, your state will vary like your trading; however, in *general*, what is your internal state of mind?

Exercise 1—Checklist of Personal Trading State

	1	2	3	4	5	
I usually trade relaxed.	O	O	O	O	O	anxious
I usually trade focused.	O	O	O	O	O	distracted
I usually trade confident.	O	O	O	O	O	unsure
I usually trade with control.	O	O	O	O	O	no control

	1	2	3	4	5	
My trading is automatic.	O	O	O	O	O	indecisive
I trade effortlessly.	O	O	O	O	O	great effort
I trade feeling energized.	O	O	O	O	O	lethargic
I trade with positive beliefs.	O	O	O	O	O	negative
I trade with positive self-talk.	O	O	O	O	O	negative
I find trading fun.	O	O	O	O	O	labored

Figure 6-2—Resourceful and Limiting Trading States

Resourceful	*Limiting*
confident	angry
enthusiastic	vengeful
energized	disappointed
disciplined	frustrated
joyful	sad
happy	stupid
knowledgeable	euphoric
loving	excited
grateful	lethargic
proud	self-doubting
having fun	disorganized
organized	indecisive
determined	confused
dynamic	anxious
vital	paralyzed
proactive	responsive

If there is one key element to the innergame that must be constantly repeated, it is this: because state of mind is the aggregate of your experiences both internal and external at any moment in time, possessing the ability to shift from an unresourceful or limiting state to one that is without limits will liberate you to achieve your trading goals. This "secret" is exactly what the top-performing traders have learned consciously over time or experience on an unconscious level. They have "learned" to master their state in order to make it work for them. Consequently, they trade relaxed, focused, confident, and in complete control at all times.

As human beings and as traders, we can relate to the world in only two ways; through our bodies (physiology) and our minds (psychology). Let's first explore the relationships between physiology and state of mind, and then, consider its implications for the innergame of trading. If you could "feel good" physically on a consistent basis, wherever and whenever you wanted—let's say while you're trading—would that make a difference in your performance? We know it would! How you are directing your physical body at any given moment dictates your capacity to achieve. Anthony Robbins has called physiology "the avenue of excellence." What he means is that knowing the specific techniques and strategies for controlling your body will determine what you are psychologically capable of achieving at any given time.

Isn't it true that your general performance suffers if you are in pain, deprived of sufficient sleep, or have a blood sugar level that is approaching the planet Pluto? And of course the opposite is also true. Peak performance results from "feeling good." Knowing how to direct your physiology will affect the quality and strength of your psychology.

Think of a time recently when you were feeling depressed, nothing major but just a little down. This memory might even have to do with a recent trading experience. Now, in your mind, see what your body looked like when you were feeling this way. Hear what you were saying to yourself. Feel what you were feeling when you were depressed. The point is, if you think about all the things you had to do when you felt depressed you'll see you really had to work at it! The following figure illustrates this point.

Figure 6-3—Feeling Depressed About a Trade

Bodily Response	Visualization	Auditory
Body feels heavy, shoulders droop, torso hunched. Facial muscles slack, breathing short and shallow. Eyes looking down. Feeling slow, bored, or unenthusiastic.	Seeing yourself fail. Watching yourself express rage or temper tantrums. Looking stupid, discouraged, hopeless.	The voice of doom, the sounds of inevitable failure. "I'm always stopped out." "Why do they always pick me off?" "Why can't I ever get it right?"

Now let's think about a time when you were really feeling confident, when you could just do no wrong. Maybe you just saw a trade, or heard something within yourself say this trade was right; or maybe it just felt like the right trade to make. Remember how it felt to be on the top of your game. You were feeling totally energized and resourceful. Figure 6-4 illustrates the internal elements of a trade that is internally represented as "feeling good."

Figure 6-4—Feeling Good About a Trade

Bodily Response	*Visualization*	*Auditory*
Body feels light, confident. Shoulders are erect, torso straight. Facial muscles taut, breathing deep and relaxed. Eyes looking up and straight ahead. Feeling strong, energized and enthusiastic.	Seeing yourself succeed. Watching yourself in control, relaxed. Looking competent, confident, positive.	The voice of confidence. The sounds of "I knew I was right." "I have the market pegged." "This market is doing just what I thought."

The point is, you can feel good about your trading whenever you want to by controlling and directing your physiology. Of course, the opposite as we have seen, is also true and that is why most traders lose the edge that makes the difference. How you experience trading then, is based on your bodily response, visualization, and what you tell yourself (auditory). That is why getting stopped out of a market, or filled above your price, or taking a profit or loss is perceived so differently among traders.

The way you employ your physiology determines your preparation and resourcefulness to trade as well as how you choose to "feel" about the experience. By doing certain specific things to your physiology (i.e., posture, bodily movements, facial expression, visual focus), you can become physically relaxed or energized. You see in gross terms the reason for this is that your physiology literally tells your mind how it should feel. I would like to illustrate this point with the following exercises.

Exercise 1

Put a smile on your face. Feel how good your facial muscles feel. Now with that big smile on your face try to get depressed. Sorry, you just can't do it. The reason is your body (facial expression) is telling your mind it feels good. Are we telling you to smile whenever you are feeling down? Yes! And of course there are other ways to improve your state as well.

So how does this relate to trading? Let me answer my question with another question. Is there any benefit to one's trading to be able to change your physical and mental state whenever you want by adjusting your physiology? I think you would have to agree the answer is an overwhelming yes. Here are some additional exercises to improve your state while trading.

Exercise 2

Go from a heavy, bored feeling to feeling energized by moving your larger muscles (arms and legs). You can accomplish this by running in place, waving your arms in a flapping motion, or strutting like a peacock. You might look silly but you'll feel great and improve the state of mind of the people who are watching you.

Exercise 3

Increase your breathing rate. Take long deep breaths in rapid succession. If you need to relax, slow down your rate of breathing and picture a calming image.

Exercise 4

Act energized. Walk around the room as if you were totally energized. See yourself in your mind as you would be if you were just brimming over with energy. Hear what you would say to yourself. Feel how it feels to be full of energy. Now double it. . . . I think you're there.

Exercise 5

Use positive self-talk. Speak with passion and enthusiasm. Frame your trading experiences in positive terms. For example, when the market stops you out compliment yourself for defining your loss.

Exercise 6

Develop your own specific moves to energize and relax yourself at work.

Now remember when you are feeling good; that is when you are in the right state of mind, your body is doing certain things, adopting a specific syntax. If you were to gauge the level of physical energy it would take to guard Michael Jordan on a scale of 1 to 10, I think you would readily agree you would have to be at least at a 10 to have a chance. Well, isn't trading as important as a game of basketball? Keep track of your personal level of physical energy and resourcefulness. Obviously, when you trade you want to be as close to 10 as possible. If you feel yourself going below 8, you're flirting with disaster.

Figure 6-5—Where Are You on a Physical Scale on a Typical Trading Day?

0 - 10

Now let's take a look at how the top traders utilize focus and belief to achieve their high level of resourcefulness, enabling them to act effortlessly with automatic responsiveness to whatever the markets present to them.

Figure 6-6—The Process of Focused Concentration

```
┌─────────────────────────────────────────┐
│  System of Empowering Personal Belief     │
└─────────────────────────────────────────┘
                    │
                    ▼
┌─────────────────────────────────────────┐
│       Resourceful Physical State;         │
│       Relaxed, Effortless Trading         │
└─────────────────────────────────────────┘
                    │
                    ▼
┌─────────────────────────────────────────┐
│        Focused Concentration on           │
│        Defined Market Phenomena           │
└─────────────────────────────────────────┘
                    │
                    ▼
┌─────────────────────────────────────────┐
│   SUCCESSFUL TRADING PERFORMANCE          │
└─────────────────────────────────────────┘
```

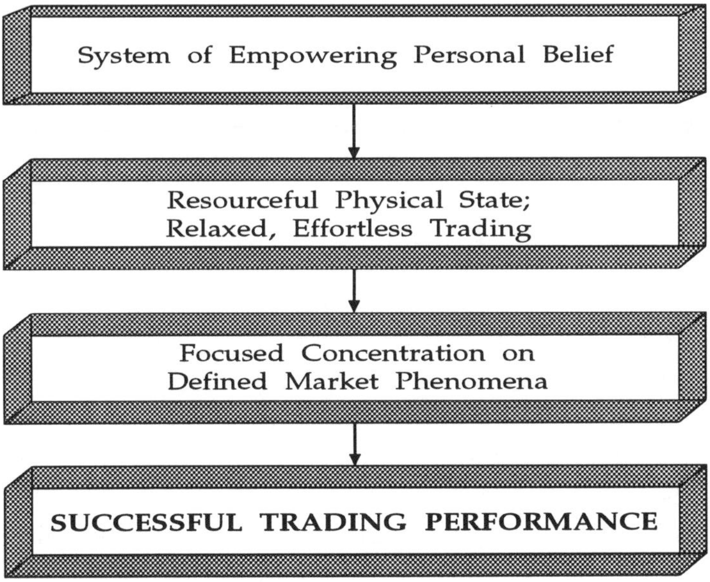

Figure 6-7—A Comparison of Focus Between Winning and Losing Traders

Winners	*Losers*
Focus is guided by a disciplined approach based on an objective market view as defined by a successful trading system.	Focus is distracted, exaggerated, omissive or in a state of denial. View is guided and dictated by near-term emotion.

Your trading focus is directed by your personal trading belief system. In general, there are three broad categories of personal trading beliefs which dictate trading performance:

1.   Universal beliefs about the market. These are global beliefs that each of us has about the market.

2.   Beliefs about ourselves. These are beliefs we have about ourselves indicating personal fear, confidence, etc.

3.   Rules to live by. We all have a system of rules. The construction in our mind is if . . . then. If I'm a successful trader then . . .

As we have seen, we all possess a host of beliefs about trading and the market. Some of these beliefs are of a purely philosophical nature while other beliefs say as much about ourselves (in terms of predicting market performance) as they do about the actual markets. If for example, you think you can never get a fair shake in the market, you are starting the game with a self-fulfilling prophecy for loss. The interesting thing about belief, however, is that it makes no difference whether your beliefs are right or wrong in an abstract sense as long as they empower you to act decisively and automatically as a trader.

Figures 6-8, 6-9, and 6-10 provide illustrations of each category of belief in its limiting and resourceful expressions.

Figure 6-8—Universal Beliefs About the Market

Limiting	*Resourceful*
"The markets are rigged."	"The markets provide opportunity."
"The market is too risky."	"This is the kind of market that requires patience."
"It's impossible to get a good fill."	"I choose to get into the market at my price."

Limiting	*Resourceful*
"The market doesn't let you win."	"The market exists to give me profits."

Figure 6-9—Beliefs About Ourselves

Limiting	*Resourceful*
"I'll never make a winning trade."	"I'll take one trade at a time."
"I'm an idiot—how could I have made that trade?"	"Everyone makes mistakes; I'll just focus on the next trade."
"What will they think about me when I tell them about this trade?""I must be perfect."	"What others think about me is not important; I'll just do my best.""I don't have to be perfect; I just have to do my best."

Figure 6-10—Rules to Live By (if . . . then)

Limiting	*Resourceful*
"If I get stopped out then I'm a loser."	"If I get stopped out then I have to reevaluate the trade."
"If the market doesn't do what I expect it to then I don't know anything."	"If the market doesn't do what I expect it to then my analysis or timing has to be reconsidered."

Limiting	*Resourceful*
"If I lose on this trade, then it's not my fault."	"If I am responsible for every market decision that I make then I'm in control."

Please complete the following exercises in order to gain a greater understanding of your personal trading belief system.

Exercise 7

Write down five beliefs that you currently have about yourself that limit your market performance.

1._____

2._____

3._____

4._____

5._____

Exercise 8

Write down five beliefs about yourself that you can adopt to improve your market performance.

1._____

2._____

3._____

4._____

5._____

Exercise 9

Write down five beliefs that you currently have about the markets or trading that limit your performance.

1._____

2._____

3._____

4._____

5._____

Exercise 10

Write down five beliefs that you can adopt about trading and the markets to enhance your performance.

1._____

2._____

3._____

4._____

5._____

Exercise 11

Write five rules (if ... then) that you currently live by as a trader.

1._____

2._____

3._____

4._____

5._____

Exercise 12

Write down five rules (if . . . then) that you can adopt to enhance your market performance.

1._____

2._____

3._____

4._____

5._____

Figure 6-11—Comparison of Belief System Between Winners and Losers

Winners	Losers
"Money is not that important."	"Money is the most important thing."
"Losing is part of the process."	"I can't lose any money."
"Trading is a game; it's fun." "I know I can win."	"Trading is serious business. I've got to trade well to pay the rent."
"There is no such thing as failure. Every setback provides me with new market information."	"I know they're going to get me—I'm going to lose again." "I'm a failure."

Figure 6-12—Comparison of Rules (if . . . then) to Live By Between Winners and Losers

Winners	Losers
"If I am to be a successful trader, then I must be patient."	"If I'm patient, then I will miss the market."
"If I get stopped out of the market, then I have learned something important."	"If I get stopped out of the market, then I'm unlucky."
"If I am a disciplined trader, then I will consistently apply my trading rules."	"If I apply my trading rules, then I won't be able to adjust to sudden market moves."
"If I take a loss, then it is part of the process."	"If I take a loss, then I am a loser."

Exercise 13

Imagine yourself having the following beliefs. As you say each belief, visualize yourself acting out this belief. Hear what it sounds like. Feel what it feels like to own this belief.

1. I believe I am going to be a successful trader.
2. I believe I am capable of achieving whatever I set my mind to do.
3. I believe I can identify and execute winning trades.
4. I believe I can trade with confidence.
5. I believe I can trade effortlessly and automatically.
6. I believe yesterday's performance has nothing to do with tomorrow's.

7. I believe I am personally responsible for all my trades.

8. I believe I can be successful without being perfect.

9. I believe my performance as a trader does not reflect my worth as a person.

10. I believe one bad trade is just *one* bad trade.

11. I believe that believing in myself and in my proven methodology at all times will give me the edge as a trader.

We have seen thus far how directing your physiology and personal belief system can give you the added competitive advantage of always trading in a winning state of mind. There is one additional element that we would like to make you aware of in order to maintain a positive state. What we would like to offer is a form of positive self-talk that we call mental calisthenics. When you ran in place or flapped your arms like a giant chicken, remember how you immediately felt energized; asking yourself certain questions will have a similar effect and will immediately improve your state of mind. The following are suggestions of the kinds of questions that can frame your internal reality at any given moment. We encourage you to come up with your own list that you can fire off in your mind at any time. Please take the time to slowly go through this list.

1. Think of something that is really good in your life. See it, hear it, feel it.

2. Think of something in your life you are really proud of. See it, hear it, feel it.

3. Think of one thing in your life that you are really grateful for. See it, hear it, feel it.

4. Think of something in your life that really excites you. See it, hear it, feel it.

5. Think of a person in your life who you love. See him/her, hear him/her, feel him/her.

6. Think of a person who loves you. See him/her, hear him/her, feel him/her.

7. Think of something that's funny. See it, hear it, feel it. How does it make you feel?

As you think about these things, be aware of the fact that your brain is your own movie theater and you're its principal actor, producer, and director. You can view any of these situations as you choose to. This is an important point because it should become obvious to you at this point you can also represent any trading experience or situation as you wish. That is why losing on a particular trade to some traders is paralyzing while to others it can be liberating or a meaningful source of additional market information.

As you make and experience these pictures, sounds, and feelings, let us point out to you some of the controls you can play with as you are creating this mental imagery. Notice what happens as you change the imagery both visually and audially in brightness, color, distance, volume, duration, etc. (See Figure 6-13.)

How you represent any single trading experience will immediately and profoundly alter your state of mind.

Figure 6-13—Internal Processes for Enhancing State

Visual	*Auditory*	*Kinesthetic (Feeling)*
Brightness	Loudness	Even
Color	Duration	Warm
Contrast	Pitch	Cold
Distance	Tone	Pulsating

Visual	Auditory	Kinesthetic (Feeling)
Location	Location	Intermittent
Shape	Direction	Strong
Size	Rhythm	Weak

Exercise 14

Think of ten visual images that can instantly change your state. Create an imaginary slide carousel in your mind so that you can tap into any single slide whenever you want to enhance your trading state. It can be an image of skydiving, bungee jumping, or winning a gold medal at the trading olympics. It's your slide show, have fun with it!

Exercise 15

Create a mini jukebox in your mind. Think of ten songs—rock, rap, classical or jazz—that you can access automatically to change your state. If the market gets you down, no problem. Fire off a tune that will keep you strong and fresh.

The words you choose to speak to yourself will also enhance or detract from your trading state. So as you perceive and interpret the market experience to yourself, be aware not only of the words you are using but how you are using them and in what internal tonality of voice.

Figure 6-14—Comparison of Negative and Positive Self-Talk

Negative Self-Talk	Positive Self-Talk
"You are a fool, how could you have made that trade?"	"Everyone makes mistakes—move on to the next trade."

Negative Self-Talk	Positive Self-Talk
"What will X think of me?"	"I'm doing my best. The good trades will take care of themselves."
"I hope I don't make a terrible trade again."	"Relax, exercise discipline, and make your next trade."
"Those floor traders picked me off again."	"I have to think more critically about where to place my stops."

Figure 6-15—Comparison of Internal Vocabulary Usage—Can You "Feel" the Difference?

Negative	Positive
idiot	disciplined
crazy	decisive
loser	patient
fool	methodical
emotional	consistent
failure	winner
wild	confident
stubborn	focused
shooter	

Remember, the top traders "know" consciously or unconsciously the role of state of mind to successful trading. Now you too know how to automatically change from a limiting to a resourceful state. Think what this will mean in every aspect of trading, from analysis to execution to closing out the trade, to be able to trade in a state of mind that is highly confident, focused, and physically relaxed where decisions are made not out of fear but effortlessly with a high degree of personal control.

The question we are now left with is how does a resourceful state of mind consistently yield trading profit? The answer to this question involves developing and matching a winning trading style and system to the specific needs of your personality.

Chapter Seven

Matching a Trading Style to Your Personality

By now, the importance of the innergame of trading in order to reach one's full potential as a trader should be quite obvious. By understanding our motives and setting goals, as well as consciously controlling our state, we can manage anxieties, focus concentration, and enhance our confidence as traders. In addition, by using specific psychological skills such as employing audio, visual, and kinesthetic (feeling) imagery, we can greatly improve our performance. Moreover, these skills will increase our level of personal enjoyment and fulfillment.

We must also consider the differences in individual personality as we think about the psychological skills we have learned and how to apply these skills when we trade markets. As individuals, each of us has specific psychological motives, goals, and tolerances that need to be factored into our choice of a trading system as well as into the development of particular strategies.

In our seminars we ask the following questions to help participants identify their strengths and weaknesses in order to assist them in selecting a trading system that fits their personality. We have learned from experience that there is no trading system that comes ready-made, one size fits all. Please take the time to answer each of the following questions:

1. What are my greatest weaknesses as a trader?

_____

_____

_____

_____

2. What are my greatest strengths as a trader?

_____

_____

_____

_____

3. What do I find most interesting about trading?

_____

_____

_____

_____

4. What do I find least interesting about trading?

_____

_____

_____

_____

5. What do I find most enjoyable about trading?

_____

_____

_____

_____

6. What do I find least enjoyable about trading?

_____

_____

_____

_____

7. How much effort (time and money) am I willing to commit to trading?

_____

_____

_____

_____

8. Is it important for me to trade by feel? Why?

_____

_____

_____

_____

9. Is it important for me to have a totally mechanical system? Why?

_____

_____

_____

_____

10. What does the ideal trading system look like to me?

_____

_____

_____

_____

As you carefully read through your responses to these questions, it should become clear to you exactly what *you* will need for your system to be successful. If you are a trader who thrives on trading by feel, a mechanical system is not what the doctor ordered and vice versa. The psychological skills you have learned up to now will greatly improve your trading performance. However, knowing the specific idiosyncrasies of your personality and temperament is the piece that will round out the ultimate success of your trading puzzle. Our attention in the next chapter is turned to the experiences and commonalities of the top traders. We will see what it is precisely that makes them so successful; how they were able to develop trading strategies that adjust to the needs of their unique personalities.

PART III

THE TOP TRADERS

Successful Trading
Demonstrated through the
Prism of Real Traders

The Innergame of Trading has a humble origin. One day in 1989, we were greeted by a trader whom we had known as a fellow member of the Chicago Mercantile Exchange. The trader was grousing about his trading that day. He described the market as particularly "hellish" and grueling. "There was just no opportunity in the market," was the way he put it. This came as something of a surprise to us because we had thought it was a great trading session. Our perception of that day's "trade" was totally different from the way our colleague had experienced it.

This chance encounter gave rise to two questions which gnawed at us over the next three years: (1) What are the common traits of successful traders? (2) Could a model of successful trading be developed and then taught to others?

As we began to study the literature on successful trading, we discovered certain broad commonsense strategies were reported over and over again as the key factors necessary for successful trading. These market rules or axioms were so general and well-known that we wondered, why is it that so few people are truly successful at trading? What also surprised us was that the more we visited with and interviewed well-known top traders, it became apparent that the motivation to make money was not the sole, significant factor correlated with one's success. The following list illustrates this point. We developed a profile of the characteristics of winning traders.

Characteristics of Winning Traders

- Money is a factor but not an essential motivation for trading.
- Trader is well-rounded in his or her personal life.
- Trader is consistent in methodology.
- Trader assumes personal responsibility for all success and failures.

- Trader is results (bottom line) oriented.

- Trader employs an automatic response to markets.

- Trader possesses flexibility and resilience.

- Trader has a positive attitude, belief system, and state of mind.

- Trader utilizes decisive decision making.

It also became readily apparent to us as we began studying successful traders that there was a specific profile of the losing trader. The following list illustrates this point.

Characteristics of Losing Traders

- Money is key.

- Trader has a narrow focus in market and personal life.

- Trader is inconsistent in approach and methodology.

- Trader refuses to accept responsibility for actions. (e.g., bad fills, choppy markets, etc.)

- Trader operates in conflict.

- Trader has a negative attitude.

- Trading is dictated by emotion.

- Trader is indecisive.

- Trader is stubborn.

We identified traders who were recognized industry-wide as top traders in order to hear from them, in their own words, what it is that they are doing differently in the market. We wanted to learn their "secrets" in order to help other traders become more successful. The traders we interviewed all had at least fifteen years of trading history. One of the traders had over

40 years of continuous trading experience; however, the average trading background was about 25 years. These individuals know every aspect of the futures industry. More than half of them had owned or operated their own clearing firms and have monitored and mentored many traders during their careers. They have a great deal to share about successful traders and successful trading.

The Traders:

Gene Agatstein

Joel Greenberg

Bruce Johnson

Leo Melamed

Jack Sandner

George Segal

Joseph Siegel

Jeffery Silverman

Donald Stevens

****

The conventional notion of successful trading is that as traders we respond to a commonly accepted reality, the market. We analyze trades, enter and exit markets, and manage our money according to the dictates of this generally accepted reality. What we have learned from the top traders and here present in *The Innergame of Trading*, is that as traders the reality (market) we respond to is our thoughts (visual, auditory, kinesthetic) and feelings (beliefs) about the market. This is to say, quite simply, that the primary reality we respond to as traders is—us! You and me. In addition, we have seen from the top traders the importance of understanding and acting according to well-formulated internal and external strategies in order to make winning trades.

Moreover, we have established that by modeling the successful "recipes" of top performers we can repeat the thoughts, feelings, beliefs, and actions of industry-recognized successful traders. In other words, if we can direct our minds and bodies in the same way the high achievers do, we can possess the core of their success and achieve similar excellent results. In an effort to understand exactly what the top performers think, feel, and believe that leads to automatic and profitable market decisions and separates them from other traders, we present the following:

The Innergame of Most Traders

- Identify market signal (i.e., point, line, etc.)
- Confused, anxious, or inconsistent reaction.
- Feel "bad" (angry, nervous, hesitant, etc.) about trade.

The Innergame of Top Traders

- Identify market signal.
- React automatically with confidence.
- Feel "good" (confident, high self-esteem, etc.) about trade.

Formula for Success

"Take the obvious, add a cupful of brains, a generous pinch of imagination, a bucketful of courage and daring, stir well and bring to a boil."

— Bernard Baruch

Chapter Eight

Motive and Motivation

Strong motivation is the common characteristic among the top traders. Motivation was identified time and time again as the key factor to achieving goals. The top traders all love to trade! It is not solely a profession; for them it is their mission. It is also viewed as an activity whose essence can not be replaced by doing something else. These traders all feel they don't "have to" trade or "should" trade, but in a very real sense, they have "chosen" to or have been "chosen" to trade. Trading from this viewpoint is appreciated as an activity of considerable enjoyment and personal fulfillment.

Leo Melamed summed it up this way:

"From the moment I entered the futures scene and opened the door to this arcane world of shouting and gesticulations, I was bewitched. The tumult; the color; the frenzy of activity; the people rushing about, shouting at the top of their voices; and acting out their mysterious incantations instantly inflamed my young and unworldly soul, awakened some unknown and uncontrollable passions from deep within, and caused me to irrevocably conclude that this, whatever it was, was for me. And so it came to pass. Although I finished law school and even successfully practiced law for some six or seven years, my heart, mind, and soul never left the world of futures . . . . "

Joel Greenberg said, "Once I discovered what was involved in trying to utilize the high leverage of futures trading, it became an intriguing situation because of supply and demand gymnastics. Once you got into a given market, it became a mystery to solve . . . not a mystery of something that's happened in the past, but a mystery of what was going to happen in the future. Since I've been a child, I've loved to put jigsaw puzzles together. For me it was more than the simple logic of trying to make the pieces fit together. The same thing holds true for the market. The idea that I would begin to talk to certain individuals who all had the same information that I had. It was interesting to hear that two or three individuals looked at it one way and someone else looked at it another way. The way the best people looked at the market was to try and put in as many variables that the other people weren't thinking about, to come up with where they thought the market was going to go. For me trading is all about the mystery of trying to figure out where the markets are going, just like a puzzle."

For Joseph Siegel "It was the challenge that attracted me to trading. I realized soon enough that trading is a game where you're going to have to compete and you better equip yourself to be able to compete aggressively with self-confidence and nerve. I loved the idea of competition, watching the eyes and overall movement of the different traders . . . learning to understand how they would react in advance and then beating them to the punch."

When we asked Gene Agatstein what first attracted him to trading he said, "I was a teenager and I saw a pretty lively over-the-counter stock market. I had a summer job with a firm and I was really impressed with how much fun everybody was having. The closest thing that I had seen to trading up until that time was sporting events, athletic encounters with winners and losers. That really appealed to me. Especially when I saw the political nature of the alternative jobs that came along. I think I was running away from politics, perhaps even away from human interaction.

"What really first attracted me to trading was the sense of independence and fun and the pure meritocratic nature of trading. You are either right or wrong and you know right away. This really appealed to me."

Chapter Nine

Successful Trading

According to Joseph Siegel, "all successful trading comes down to three things, "knowledge, nerve, and the ability to lose money."

"Everybody has the ability to lose money but it takes nerve to lose and then choose to stay in the game . . . to want to come back . . . to have the audacity to assume that you're smart enough and quick enough to make your trade and take advantage of opportunities and make money. I found that the psychology of being able to lose money and come back was a big factor. Because it's very easy to lose money and very easy to become discouraged. You have to have a great deal of confidence in yourself that even though you've taken a beating in the market, whatever form it takes, you can come back, you can return and trade effectively.

"I remember many years ago in an egg market. It was January eggs and Van Hess had control of the egg market. Probably not only in January but in December. Every day the market was limit bid. The way you got your bid on the board—it was black board trading at that time—you put your name in a hat and whoever's name was called got the first line of bid. Well at a certain point my brother had told me that the next morning I was to sell out the entire egg position that we owned. So the next morning I got first in line on the bids but instead of selling out the position I put in more bids. I was bullish.

"Van Hess then sold all the limit bids. And the market started to cascade down and locked limit down. Needless to say I got hurt very badly but I learned from that experience. By overcoming my mistakes and having the nerve to come back, the self-confidence to come back, I knew I could make it."

Donald Stevens advised, "You must define certain parameters. Frequently when I get to a point when I enter a market I can't see the market going too much against me or I'm out. You must have a strict code which you can apply with discipline. You must act consistently and decisively."

Gene Agatstein said, "Successful trading gets right down to the psychology of self-esteem and confidence. If you're trading long enough and intensely enough, I think ultimately the statistics have to work in your favor if you just hold on to the winners and cut the losers. So why doesn't it work for everyone? The answer is self-confidence.

"I also think it's kind of hard to disentangle money management from this whole issue of self-esteem and self-confidence. If you're thinking dollars and cents on each trade whether you're right or wrong, the amount of money can be very intimidating. I think everybody overtrades a little bit. Overreaches when they feel good. They get a little bit too committed to a position. If you're unlucky enough to get hit, you could be out of business. But for me, in order to make money, I believe you have to be willing to risk your trading capital. I've always felt that if I'm in the market and adequately capitalized—I'll sit down with a pencil and paper and figure out how much I can lose on this trade—where I think the trade can go against me and how much that would translate into dollar losses. I think my strongest and best performances have been when I've in fact lost money on a trade initially and been tested to that point. When the market's turned around and left me in my trade. I always feel they can't hurt me anymore. They hurt me and I survived and now I'm riding the right way with the market. It's that sort of snapping back, that sense of being down money and then finding yourself back in the game."

George Segal put it this way: "I think that successful traders have a personality, that they're not afraid to have nineteen losing trades out of twenty, because the twentieth can be a trade that's much greater than all the nineteen put together. They're not hung up on losing money. They want to protect what they've got and wait for the opportunity to make a lot of money.

"They're willing to accept the loss, to take a loss and come back and make another trade, and know there's always tomorrow. There's always another trade to be made tomorrow. They don't like to take a big loss.

"The only thing I think about when I make a trade, I'm never thinking about how much I'm going to make. I'm always concerned about where I'm going to get out if I'm wrong.

"Money management is probably the most important thing, I would say. Whether it's 100 thousand or 10 million dollars. What holds most traders back is not being able to admit they're wrong. I think a lot of people have trouble admitting they've made a mistake, that this is not the right time. The timing was off, or the market's not ready. Maybe there are other factors in this market you don't know about. They're just not willing to admit that they're wrong.

"There are also people who are afraid to go into trades, but they shouldn't be trading if they're afraid to get involved, even if it's only a one lot. I mean I would assume a lot of people have gotten out of trading because they're afraid to make trades.

"Another thing. Everybody can get out of a winning trade. It's pretty easy to get out of a winning trade. But most people get out of a winning trade much too soon. But it's very hard to get out of a losing trade. When I'm in a trade I'm looking to see how far the market can go and where I think it can go. I'm looking to maximize. I try—I do have a target when I go into it and I try not to pay too much attention to the market while it's going good. I don't like watching every tick. Many times the best markets I've ever had were markets that I've added to the positions, bull positions on strength and bear positions on weakness. Because I feel convinced now that the market has corroborated my thinking, that it's now going to do what I thought it would do.

"I want to make a very important point. I try not to think about the market when I leave the office. Of course, this is not easy to do. Frustration, annoyance, aggravation. If it bothers me enough, I'll get out of the market. Many times I have gotten out of losing positions because it just bothered me too damn much. It just bothered me, where I couldn't sleep or where—I don't get depressed, but where it's just bothered me outside of work to the point where I—feel much better when I get out. Getting out of a losing trade is an uplifting feeling to me. It's not as uplifting as getting out of a winning trade, but it really takes the burden off your shoulders. To have to sit with that loser and die with that loser is crushing. Just get out. When you can't sleep or when it affects your life, you've got to do something about it. It's very easy just to pick up the telephone and say 'good-bye!' "

According to Joel Greenberg, "Successful trading requires an awful lot of tenacity. You have to have powers of conviction that you're right. When you then begin to put your money where your mouth is, you must make your investment within your means.

"Many people in the speculative world figure that when they buy or sell, they're going to be immediately right, which to me is ridiculous. It's a bad psychology. I figure I'm going to be immediately wrong. If you take that psychology and you enter a market with the idea that you're not buying the absolute low, then you're going to have to continue to buy as the market goes lower and you can do that if your convictions are there. If you don't have those convictions, I mean, I can go into a market and buy and I know I'm not going to have to go and buy again. But when I buy the second and third time, I begin to change my mind, I lose my tenacity. I lose my conviction. If at that point I feel that I'm not comfortable, then I'll begin to exit. But, if I feel I'm right, if I have the conviction then I'll stand through the market going against me. So tenacity's the word.

"You must understand and know everything you can about the market you're going to be investing in. Otherwise, you're at someone else's whim. You must also have the conviction that you're right until the market proves you wrong. I have to know every fundamental and psychological factor that's going to be affecting my market.

"Psychologically, I've noticed something very interesting from customers and you can apply this to almost any speculator. When a speculator is wrong, he almost always likes to hide from the fact. So, he lets his losses drag because he doesn't want to face up to the fact that he may be wrong and believes somehow tomorrow's going to be different. So, many of your losers look at markets that way. Also, the same people that feel that they don't want to face up to the fact that they're losing "internally" don't even want to call in and find out how the market's doing. On the other hand, when they're making money, psychologically, they can't wait to tell the next person. They can't wait to take the profit. So, there again, they take their profits much too soon. They watch the market like a hawk when they're making X dollars and they get out as soon as they think they've got an excellent winner. The truth of the matter is, in many cases when you've got a winner, you better stick with it because maybe this market will run a lot longer than people think.

"The first market I ever ventured into, I really didn't know anything about it except I had some supply and demand figures in front of me. It was the cotton market. That's the one that I bought my membership from. I just read the supply and demand factors and it came in correct. Then, I started to apply the same fundamentals to the bellies and later on to the hogs and cattle markets. What really did it for me was being right two or three markets in a row. Then, you begin to get the confidence, not only that you're right, but if I'm right on small positions, why can't I be right on larger positions? So it begins to feed on itself. Of course, that can be your downfall too.

"Psychologically, you can also feel that you cannot be wrong. Some people would say that happened to me, but I feel that I just—many times when I'm wrong in the market, it comes from external forces which I've never been able to ascertain to begin with. For example, if you get long in the belly market, and all of a sudden the government comes out with a nitrite scare, you can be wrong for 20 cents in the market and get killed, but fundamentally, you were right. You were right but you didn't have any money to take home when you were through! Or there can be a threat of a war or some climatic condition that can come up quite suddenly that you don't anticipate. A tremendous snow storm in a particular area which was never forecast.

"The other external force that can prove you wrong too is that we have to rely on many different sources for information. One of them is the government. Of course, everybody gets the same government figures at the same time. But the government makes some big mistakes. Of course, I do a lot of my trading off of what I feel are the government numbers. If the government numbers are wrong, then I'm going to be wrong. When I know that I'm wrong and in a bad position, I definitely have to make a move. Everyday I have to do something in the direction to get myself out. If I'm wrong and I have to get out of 10 percent in a day, at least it's something, so I'm doing something. Whenever

I feel I'm wrong, I must make a move to lighten my position. I just can't go the other way and I can't turn away from it, so I force myself.

"The major problem that I have when I'm wrong from a fundamental basis is that I overstay. I will look back in retrospect and say, 'Why didn't I start on X date rather than at X plus Y.' That's very difficult. In retrospect to pound yourself on the head is not fair. But, I do try to critique myself to learn from each experience."

Chapter Ten

Words of Advice

Gene Agatstein had this to say about trading:

"Trading can be incredibly difficult. Having to listen to yourself all the time, having to bounce these ideas off yourself, having to internalize all of these emotions, and having to draw on yourself for strength all the time, psychologically. But I know also it's very exciting and rewarding. Philosophically, many times I wonder how valuable is this? Is this really maximizing human potential, to confine oneself to this one specific arena of activity? It's so intense, more so, I think, than most careers, in that you don't have the interaction with other people in accomplishing objective goals. So I suppose, as far as advice, I would bring these things up to a young trader and have him think about it before he's drowning in his own emotions in the market. The notion of reminding the trader that there is always another day, another opportunity, and never forgetting, also, that trading can be so rewarding and so enjoyable."

Joseph Siegel advised, "Any trader would greatly benefit by learning how to teach himself to become more confident. Confidence comes from a belief in oneself based on hard work and disciplined trading. Do not overtrade! Start slow and work your way up and don't be jealous of the other traders; it makes no difference what the others are doing! If you learn to understand yourself you've got an edge on everyone else."

Joel Greenberg underscored this point. "When you finally pick out the market or markets that you think you want to trade, before you really go in and put your money down on the line, learn as much about that market as you can. I can say in retrospect, that it is essential to learn the fundamentals as much as you can. Once you have learned the fundamentals you must also be cognizant of what the technicians are doing. You've got a whole ball of wax here. You know what? You don't have to be a pro in every market. All you really have to do is pick out, for example, the gold market or the stock market. Any distinct commodity. You just learn as much as you can about it. Corn, soybeans, you may not turn up to be the world's biggest winner, but I bet you will win more times than you lose if you have conviction and confidence in order to act out on your knowledge."

****

The following interviews are presented here in their entirety to illustrate how four of the top traders responded in detail to many of the psychological issues raised in *The Innergame of Trading*. The reason we have selected these traders is that, in our opinion, their ideas are representative of the opinions and characteristic of the approach of all the top traders. These interviews clearly demonstrate the depth of knowledge and experience that the top traders possess, and reaffirm the idea that by utilizing the psychological skills that they have mastered, any serious trader can measurably improve his or her own trading.

Chapter Eleven

Leo Melamed

Leo Melamed is chairman emeritus of the Chicago Mercantile Exchange and is an active futures trader and chairman and CEO of Sakura Dellsher Inc., a futures commission merchant. In his first term as chairman of the CME from 1969 to 1971, Mr. Melamed was instrumental in pioneering the concept of foreign currency futures and in creating the International Monetary Market—the first futures market for financial instruments. Mr. Melamed was chairman of the IMM until its merger with the CME in 1976, when he became chairman of the combined institution. Mr. Melamed is the former chairman of the GLOBEX Corporation, which, beginning in 1990, became the unified electronic system for the Chicago Board of Trade and the CME. He has been an advisor to the Commodity Futures Trading Commission and has lectured and written extensively on the subject of financial futures markets. Mr. Melamed is the editor of An Anthology: The Merits of Flexible Exchange Rates *and the author of* Leo Melamed on the Markets.

****

Q: *Leo, what first attracted you to trading?*

LEO: Things happen by virtue of circumstance to a great extent. I wandered into the world of butter and eggs in the '50s, not even knowing that it existed. So, I can't say to you that I always planned to be a trader because that would have been the furthest thing from my mind. I planned to be a lawyer. But there was an immediate fascination. . . .

I've often wondered over the years why I understood so quickly and easily the principles of supply and demand. I've concluded that it is by virtue of an economics teacher that I had in high school. Her name was Ms. Wheelock. This teacher made me sit up and listen. She made economics exciting. I've come to the conclusion that a lot of the rudimentary things I learned about markets—what makes them go up and down, supply and demand, and so on—I learned from this teacher. How much can you get in one Econ class in high school? Well, you can get quite a bit if you have the right teacher. Luckily, I did.

Q: *So when you first arrived in the world of butter and eggs in the '50s you possessed just a rudimentary understanding of trading?*

LEO: Yes, but that wasn't sufficient when I finally became seriously interested in markets. Then I began a lot of personal study. In fact, I did do an awful lot of formal reading as if I was studying in a course in economics. Then, in the early '60s—When I started being serious about trading, I really wanted to know everything that anybody had ever written that was worthwhile. That's when I first encountered the writings of Milton Friedman. Through those readings, it became obvious to me that he was the most informed authority in economics I had ever run across. His logic was impeccable. That's what attracted me. Ultimately, Milton Friedman became my personal god in economics. He still is to this day. I think he is the brightest free-thinking mind in economics, in our time. Adam Smith was probably that before him, but I didn't know him; I knew Friedman.

Q: *So, it would be fair to say Milton Friedman has greatly influenced your understanding of markets?*

LEO: Yes, in fact, in later years, I would go to his lectures at the University of Chicago whenever I could, even though I wasn't enrolled. Wherever he was speaking, I would go.

Q: *What else do you feel prepared you for trading?*

LEO: A lot of reading, a lot of listening.

Q: *People love the economics side, like you, and you obviously had developed a real interest in it. How did you make the transition from wanting to understand the economic side of markets in an intellectual sense, to the actual trading, which, as you know, is a transition most people don't make?*

LEO: For me, the trading probably came first. Economic lessons came later. I was attracted to trading the moment I walked in on the floor and saw the frenzy and the color and the tumult. For me it was like sex. It was an instantaneous love affair between me and whatever the hell it was, but I didn't know what it was when I first saw it as a runner on the Merc. I clearly didn't understand exactly what they were doing. But, I got the feeling that whatever it was, I wanted to do it. So much so that it easily overtook my feelings for the law. Trading quickly became my number one mistress in a very short order. No sooner could I lay my hands on a couple of hundred dollars, I began to trade, not successfully, but I began to trade. The attraction was instant. It was a magnet. It hit some responsive cord inside of me. I was drawn to the challenge of figuring it out, of knowing when to buy and when to sell. It wasn't simply the money that it represented; it was the challenge of being right; you only kept *score* in money. It's trying to be right that, in fact, fuels me to stay with this game even today.

I have a chapter in my book *Leo Melamed on the Markets*, "Be a Lover, not a Fighter." That has been my credo. A lover means somebody that follows the market, loves the market, loves to be on the right side of the market. A fighter is someone who wants to be right over and above what the market tells him to be. I mean, his way is the way. The only way! Well, his way isn't necessarily the right way. The right way is the way the market wants to go. You have to know the difference! You have to know that distinction between the lovers and the fighters. I tried to be a lover. It took me a long time to learn that lesson. I can't say that I was successful off the bat because I wasn't. I think I went broke three times before I succeeded. Going broke in those days didn't take a lot.

Q: *But you came back for more?*

LEO: I came back because I loved trading. I'd come back because practicing law provided an income stream. What attracted me was simply that—let me try and put it in words. I recognized that in the market, I had ultimate democracy. By that I mean that the market will respond to the ultimate votes of supply and demand. Not by virtue of a tip someone might give you. Not by virtue of what someone else thinks the market might do. The market is going to go up when there's more buyers. It's going to go down when there's more sellers. That's pure democracy to me. It's the vote of reality. Reality is always voting. That's why, by the way, throughout the years, if you remember my history, I always fought against the corners and the squeezes and the manipulations because that was trying to distort reality. I love the reality of the market. That pure moment when price is established, on the basis of supply and demand. Free, simple and true. It is for only a moment because the next moment a new seller, a new buyer would change that value. A new fact, new information, was constantly coming, constantly changing the market's opinion of value. That's fine.

But, each seperate moment of time represents true value. That, to me, is beautiful.

Q: *And you saw this "beauty" as an opportunity?*

LEO: Yes. I saw that it was up to me to figure out how supply and demand would effect the ultimate price; how I would analyze market conditions, events, and the psychology of other traders was the challange; but this made the challange worthwhile.

Q: *Did you view trading as a personal competition?*

LEO: A challenge.

Q. *What about as competition with other people?*

LEO: Figuring out where the market was going was the challenge. In figuring out where the market was going, you clearly had competition. Others were trying to figure out the same thing and others had different opinions. In the pit you have an environment where everybody's a competitor. What you had to do with your competition is you had to know what they were thinking, what were their positions. You had to figure out how much they bought and sold and know their tolerance levels: how much could they buy before they had to sell? How much could they sell before they had to buy? How far would they let the market go against them before they admitted defeat?

These were the competitive considerations of a pit trader. But, at the end of the day none of that would do you any good if you were wrong in the market. In other words, if you correctly estimated supply and demand, nothing else mattered. So, yes, I took into consideration the competitive forces around me. But, I always kept trying to figure out where I thought the market would go on the basis of its true value.

Q: *Having expressed the influences on your own development as a trader, what in your opinion, does it take to become a successful trader?*

LEO: I've been asked that a thousand times. There is no clear answer. I think it's the psychological makeup of the person more than anything else. Clearly, if you're trained to be a trader it helps. If you're educated, it helps. If you've got money, it helps. If you're tall and got good elbows in the pit, it helps. But, all of those things don't help enough! The main element is you're own psychological makeup! It has to be a psychology that allows you not to have any ego. A person with ego cannot be a successful trader. Because there are times that you are wrong! If your ego prevents you from saying and admitting to yourself, "I am wrong," then you'll be defeated, you'll lose, you will go broke! You have to have a personality that is always honest with yourself. You cannot be influenced by what someone else is doing. "Maybe he knows things I don't know and he's buying so I should be buying," that's not how you become a good trader.

Q: *A good trader must have a personality that is always honest with himself?*

LEO: Yes, a good trader has to be honest with himself. What do I believe is the central question? Do I believe that this market's going up? Do I believe this market's going down? On the basis of what I see, on the basis of what I know, I have to be honest with myself. If that opinion is wrong, I have to admit it to myself as quickly as possible. It's a psychology of wanting to win. Wanting to be right and being willing to admit defeat to yourself in order that you can be right the next time.

Q: *What other psychological characterisitcs of personality do you think successful trading requires?*

LEO: It requires a risk taker's mentality. I mean, there are people who simply cannot take a risk. They have to put their money into Treasury bills; they want their interest and that's all.

Q: *What do you think are the primary psychological barriers that prevent most traders from being successful?*

LEO: One of them is the ability to take a loss. You've got to know that no risk taker is going to be right all the time. As a matter of fact, I figured out when I was trading that I could be wrong 60 percent of the time and come out a big winner. The key is money management. You must take your losses quickly and keep them small and let your profits run and make them worthwhile. In that fashion, you could be wrong 60 percent of the time and have a big result because you'll make a lot more money the 40 percent of the time that you are right.

Q: *In your experience what holds people back?*

LEO: A lot of people just can't face the fact that they're wrong. So, you need these two elements. First of all, the willingness to take a risk. And the other thing is the ability to admit that you are wrong. There is also a third element. You must isolate your emotions. Don't let the emotion of a loss carry over to your next trade because then you'll surely ruin the next trade!

Each trade has to be independent on its own. You cannot let a previous defeat affect the next attempt. If you do you've got a mission to vindicate your previous loss. That should never be the psychology of a trader. Each trade has to stand on its own merits; on its own two feet and once it's over, it's over.

Q: *Some people have difficulty taking the profits?*

LEO: Letting the profits run is another kind of problem. But, keeping the losses small and being willing to take a loss is much more difficult. And most important, you must learn not to allow a loss or a series of losses to defeat you.

Q: *What was the biggest psychological barrier for Leo Melamed to overcome as a trader?*

LEO: I don't know that there was just one. I think not becoming obsessed with my opinion was to me the biggest threat and one that I consistently violated over the years. So, I know that I didn't always adhere to the best principles of successful trading. I would become imbued with a view and sometimes ended up fighting a market or fighting the tape, as they say. That was my most difficult psychological barrier.

Q: *How about ego?*

LEO: I had less of a problem with that. You know, I don't believe I even have an ego problem today. The press likes to attribute one to me, but it's not true. I know myself pretty well.

Q: *You know, everyone goes through difficult periods when they trade. You just spoke about psychological barriers that you had to overcome to develop into a winning trader. When you're going through a difficult period, what do you say to yourself? What are you thinking? What do you visualize? What do you feel, emotionally and physically?*

LEO: The danger is that the difficult period will throw off your rules and logic. You've got to have a set of rules, whether it's instinctive rules or written rules. Every good trader has that set of rules. I've said a good trader is like a Stradivarius violin. You can play beautiful music on it, but if it's out of tune, even a little bit out of tune, the music isn't very good. In order to be that Stradivarius and continue to be successful, to be on your game, so to speak, you have to stay in tune. When you go through a difficult period, you get out of tune. Suddenly, something emotionally is wrong with your thinking and that starts a process where suddenly your logic gets distorted.

Q: *Your logic gets distorted?*

LEO: Yes, you forget your rules. You violate principles that you know are correct. Suddenly, your whole structure of trading comes apart —you're now doing things that you shouldn't be doing. If you think about it, you're reacting to emotions that you normally wouldn't react to. In other words, the Stradivarius is out of tune. That's the experience that every trader has encountered in one fashion or another.

Q: *What are you saying to yourself at those times?*

LEO: Sometimes you just have to get out of the position. It's no good nursing the position that is causing this distortion in your trading. I've learned that for me, I have to get out. I have to clean the slate. I have to get away from that particular position. Even if it's for only a day or two or three, sometimes a week. But, I have to get away. I have to have a mental cleansing of the slate so that I can be in the right state of mind and look at that market fresh the next time.

Q: *Do you ever say to yourself, "Leo, that was a dumb thing to do"?*

LEO: Thousands of times. There is no good trader alive that doesn't do dumb things. In fact, you've got to be able to admit to yourself when you're wrong. You did a dumb thing. You didn't listen to the warning signal. You violated your own rules. These are dumb things that you did and you've got to do smart things. You've got to be honest with yourself.

Q: *When you are talking to yourself is there an emotional feeling attached to this self-talk? Or are you just intellectualizing, verbally, with yourself?*

LEO: You have to get the emotions out of the way. You have to strip yourself from emotions and you have to intellectualize. The emotions should not be anywhere near your decision-making process. Emotional reactions are the worst reasons to make a trade or make a decision. That was my strongest asset; an ability to remove personal emotion from a market decision. Whenever I let emotion dictate, I had to clean the slate, get out of the market, step away from the trade, and regain my equilibrium.

Q: *When you're making a decision to step out of the market, to get out of it, and make a clean slate, are you visualizing things like the money? Do you see the numbers of the debit on your P & S?*

LEO: If you do, it's all the more reason to get out. If your reason for staying with the position is because you can't emotionally stand the financial loss, then you know it's the wrong position. That's when you must get out! Because until you do that, you will not be able to think clearly. You've got to face that loss. You've got to literally see and feel it. You know what I used to do? When I traded in the pit I forced this habit on myself. At the end of every day I would go through all my trades and calculate the bottom line. How did I come out that day? I'd write it down, day by day, my profit and loss. The profit didn't matter to me, but the loss side, to know that I took this loss and see it in writing and feel it with my own handwriting. It was a very important discipline.

Q: *What do you see and what do you feel and what do you hear when things are going great for you? What do you tell yourself then?*

LEO: Well, it's a huge high. It's indescribable. There have been those who equate it to sex.

Q: *Euphoric?*

LEO: Yes, it's euphoric. And, as a matter of fact, it is sexual. I think it physically drains you. It's very much like an orgasm that you have in a physical sense. It is very comparable to making love. So, it's an enormous high. The danger is not to allow it to affect other aspects of your life. I was always very careful that it shouldn't. That is, in terms of how you treat other people. What you do in your personal life, in your family, the things you buy or don't buy.

You know when I used to buy a present for myself? When I was a loser, not when I was a winner. I would go out when I had a series of losses and we all have them ... when I felt particularly defeated, I would go out and buy something expensive to show myself that I could still afford it.

Q: *I'm glad you said that. I used to take my wife out for dinner on a bad day.*

LEO: Yes, when I had a good day, I would very seldom reward myself. Because discipline required that I stay within my limits of life, irrespective of my victories in the market. I tried to keep reins on that. A lot of people don't. But, you have to learn not to let the high of winning adversely affect your daily dealings with human beings so that you don't lord it over anybody. There's a tendency to do that.

Q: *Could you express the full range of emotions that you feel in the markets, and specifically, what do you do to change your state of mind?*

LEO: There is an enormous range of emotions. They go from euphoria to depression. Just so you understand, I believe very strongly that at the end of the trading day, you should put it all away like in a drawer. You should close the drawer on all those emotions, and walk away from it. You should let your normal life take over. That is the healing process. Not to let the losses dictate my state of mind nor the profits was key to normalcy.

Q: *Is that the way you change your state of mind if you are feeling depressed about a trade or a series of trades?*

LEO: Absolutely.

Q: *You make a conscious effort to walk out the door and say, "I can't do anything about it until tomorrow morning"?*

LEO: I couldn't always accomplish this within the same minute that I wanted it done. But, I knew that I was on the track of doing that and that within an hour or so, after it was over, it was over! I closed it up until tomorrow. Tomorrow I'd open that drawer and take another look. That, in itself, is a healing process.

Q: *Did you ever say anything to yourself?*

LEO: Sure. You have to say it to yourself; you compartmentalize; remember, it's over. Finished. Walk away from it! On to the next one! When you say that to yourself you take charge. You're in control.

Q: *What are some of the beliefs you have of yourself as a trader?*

LEO: To begin with number one you've got to have faith in yourself. If you don't have faith in yourself, you cannot be a successful trader. You cannot be a trader who thinks of himself as a loser. If you do you're surely going to lose. You've got to feel that you're a winner. As long as you feel that you're a winner, you'll have a chance. That doesn't mean that you will always be a winner! But, at least you have the right psychology. You've got to believe in yourself. You've got to believe that you know what you're doing. You've got to believe that your opinion is of value, that you're qualified to have an opinion. That's the psychology that you must have.

Q: *Any other beliefs?*

LEO: You must be consistent and decisive.

Q: *Did you have a mentor or role model who you feel helped you become a better trader?*

LEO: Well, to tell you the truth, I had a number of role models.

Q: *Did they help you become a better trader?*

LEO: I think so. They all taught me something. Each one of them was in his own way a great trader. There was a guy, Sydney Shear, who traded potatoes in New York. He was one fabulous trader in the early days of potatoes. You know, when Maine potatoes was the big thing in the New York market. The only reason I knew him—I was a kid—was because I knew his son. His son and I were friends. And, Sydney, the father, taught me something that I never forgot. He taught me, that if you want to know how strong a market is, walk in to start selling, even if you want to buy. Find out if the market can take your sales, particularly if you were a well-known personality like he was in potatoes. So, I would see him, knowing that he was going into buy; watch him really sell with a vengence just to see if the market took his sales and held its price structure. If it did, he knew it was right to buy. Then, he would have brokers or somebody else go in and buy for him. That was his test of market strength and vice versa when he wanted to sell.

Q: *I would suspect that would be psychologically very difficult for many people to do?*

LEO: I suppose so, but it's certainly a logical way to test how strong or weak the market is. After all, if you start to sell and the market falls apart, maybe you shouldn't be buying. Maybe this is a reason not to buy because the market's a lot weaker than you thought. So, it really does serve a very important purpose. Sydney Shear taught me that. He was certainly a role model for me.

Another guy that taught me a great deal is somebody you've probably heard of and knew, Ralph Peters. Ralph Peters was a role model for me because what he taught me is something that I really wasn't in tune with. I was a short-term trader. Remember, we were pit traders. Pit traders are short-term, very short-term. Five minutes, three minutes, a day is a long time!

Ralph Peters taught me that the real big money is not made that way. He showed me that if you really have views about the market, long-range views; you could really capitalize on this conviction. Ralph was a guy that would stay in a position for months, even for years. He had the long-range view of things. Soybeans were going up to $12 a bushel, and so what you had to do was put on a position at $6 and stay for the next $6. Or, until such time as you were convinced they were not going to $12. That is the long-range view of things.

For a short-term trader, like I was at the time, to think about long-term was the difference between day and night. It represented an entirely new world of discovery for me! Ralph, in his way, taught me to think about the longer term. It changed my style.

Later in time, when I left the floor because I was chairing the exchange, I had to give up the pit. I had to be upstairs, I had to be on the phones and so forth. So, I had to learn to play the game from afar, and therefore, from long-range. I couldn't trade in and out, as a pit trader. It was Ralph Peters that taught me about how to go about thinking about the long term. That doesn't mean you were going to be right all the time, but it forced me to think in the long term.

Q: *Many traders have a lot of difficulty watching a market move their way and knowing that even though they have so much more potential long term, just having to watch the market come off in a natural market reaction, is psychologically very difficult for them to do.*

LEO: Yes, that's right; that's where conviction comes in. You've got to have a lot of faith in your opinion to do that. Let me say that again. You have to have a lot of faith in yourself and your ability. You've got to know what danger signals are. Markets naturally retrace and you've got to be willing to withstand those backs and fills.

But, you've got to know what is a retracement and what is a reversal. Sometimes a reversal is a danger signal, a warning signal to which one should pay attention. Those are things you learn over time. In terms of role models, certainly Ralph Peter's kind of thinking was a role model for me. Another guy that taught me quite a bit was Roy Simmons, a very successful trader.

Q: *Wonderful man.*

LEO: Yes, a wonderful guy and a wonderful trader. Roy was involved in everything under the sun. I once took a look at what he was doing. I mean, he was in everything. Well, that taught me that you can monitor more than one position at a time. I think there should be a limit to that. I don't think everybody is Roy Simmons. But, at least you could go beyond the one single commodity at a time. Roy also taught me that there were relationships among commodities. Because he wasn't always long everything or short everything. At some things he was short, at some things he was long. So, I recognized from that that you can use the spread values of being short and long to assist your overall plan. In some ways, it helped me manage the risk better.

Q: *Do you think you can be over-diversified in your choice of positions?*

LEO: That is true. I always maintain that three or four positions was all that I ever really wanted, at a time. But, I saw Roy Simmons and he certainly led me to go beyond being a single product trader. I also learned from someone else who had enormous influence on me and taught me some of the basic principles about trading. He taught me that there are two approaches to the market. The technical approach and the fundamental approach. It was Elmer Faulkner who was my teacher with respect to a technical approach to trading. Here was a guy that in his day had made and lost many millions of dollars. At the time I met him, he was broke again. Nevertheless, he had an enormous understanding about the technicals and an uncanny ability to read charts. He led me to eventually read and study everything about technical trading. In fact, I became enamored with the ideas of technical trading.

On the other hand, I learned from a guy you know very well, Marlow King, that fundamentals ultimately decide the market's true value. There's no question supply and demand are the ultimate determinants of where the market is going. The main point from Marlow King's perspective was that ultimately, a market will go where the supply and demand dictates. So, all you need to do is be able to figure out what the supply and demand looks like statistically to determine where the market's going. That was his approach. He didn't care about technicals. So, in essence I learned from the two of them. They were both my role models. They were as diverse role models as you could possibly have, because each of them viewed the market quite differently. Elmer Faulkner couldn't give a damn about supply and demand. It didn't matter. All that you had to do was read the charts, read the charts!

Q. *What is the answer, Leo?*

LEO: My answer is that, first of all, there's no such thing as a pure technician or pure fundamentalist. In today's world, the good trader is probably a little of both. Traders have to know what the fundamentals are, and they surely ought to know what the technicals say. It's when you have a combination of the two that mesh that you're going to make some money. So, one ought to know both. That's what I learned. The other thing I learned is that what Marlow King was trying to do with fundamentals is very hard to do because supply and demand is constantly changing. It is very difficult to keep up with all that goes into supply and demand. It's not a simple statistic. It's made up of a myriad of facts. Also, you have to know the relative importance of each of those statistical flows. Sometimes demand is more important than supply. Sometimes there are other extraneous factors. In other words, you don't know what relative percentages of importance to attribute to each factor. So, it is never a simple formula.

There are new informational flows every day. Every week. Every month. It's very hard to track all of that. Few people can do it. I couldn't do it!

On the other hand, what I could do is learn how to read the chart. When I say chart, I mean the technical approach. The chart, after all, takes into account what all participants in the markets are doing. Right? The buys and sales of the participants in the market create the chart. So, therefore, the chart is representative of every trader.

So you have a complete picture of all the Marlow Kings and all the Elmer Faulkners, because all their buys and sales result in making those lines on the chart. So, if you could interpret that you, in fact, can interpret all of the fundamentals. That's the logic of technical interpertation. It is not voodoo. It's simply a sum total of everybody's opinion in the marketplace. Ergo, in theory it should work. For example, if you go into a crowded theater and shout fire, the people are going to get up from their seats and run for the exits. It's a conditioned response. Well, charts and technical interpertations are representative of the same kind of thing. They create patterns that can be interpreted.

If you learn all of that and interpret it well, you can use the technical end of the market without knowing that much about the fundamental. But, as I said at the outset, it's better to know a little bit about the fundamentals as well. My approach, therefore, over the years, is 60-65 percent technical, 30-35 percent, maybe 40 percent, fundamental. But generally speaking I don't make any real money unless my technical interpertation is in sync with my fundamental opinion.

Q: *I used to tell a story in seminars. It could be any commodity, but I'd say I know two people in the world, the only two people in the world who really know anything about gold, and one's Long and one's Short.*

Finally, Leo, what would you say to somebody who is interested in becoming a successful trader? What words of advice or encouragement might you offer to somebody who is genuinely committed to making it as a trader in the futures markets?

LEO: It's the biggest challenge you're ever going to have. It's the most interesting challenge around. It's both a vocation and an avocation because it's all-consuming! And the rewards justify the risks.

But there's no nine to five to it. It's a twenty-four hour occupation. You're never out of the markets. You're never out of tune. You're in tune with the world all of the time. I would say it's a great attraction for someone who has the right psychology and the right personality. And you must have risk capital, so that if you lose, it won't change your lifestyle. If you can succeed, it is a wonderful experience.

I would caution however that there's an enormous downside to trading. You may not succeed. It's very difficult. Don't consider yourself a failure if you don't succeed. Because you might succeed in many other walks of life. If you can't succeed in trading, it doesn't mean you can't be successful in other things. The other downside is that if you do succeed, you're going to have a very short life. Absolutely a much shorter life, but I don't mean in physical years. You're still going to live the same amount of years that you would in any other profession you might have chosen. But, the time will move much quicker as a trader. Your day, week, month zips by. It's so exciting. It's so interesting that days are shorter, life is shorter. That's unfortunate. You live the same number of years as your friend down the street that worked in the office, but he had a longer life!

Q: *But he thinks of his life as drudgery.*

LEO: Maybe.

Q: *This is the ultimate entrepreneurial trip. Isn't it?*

LEO: Yes. Absolutely.

Chapter Twelve

John F. (Jack) Sandner

In January 1993, Jack Sandner began a record ninth year as chairman of the Chicago Mercantile Exchange (CME). The first chairman in CME history elected to a two-year term under rules approved by the Board of Governors in 1991, he represents more than 2,700 members and 90 member firms. First elected CME chairman in 1980, Mr. Sandner remained chairman for three consecutive terms through 1982, after which he served three years as the board-appointed legislative liaison. He was elected chairman again in 1986 and re-elected for two more terms through 1988. In 1989 and 1990, he served as senior policy advisor before being elected chairman once again in 1991.

A pivotal industry leader, Mr. Sandner played a critical role in the development of GLOBEX, the international after-hours, electronic trading system. In April 1993, he was appointed chairman of GLOBEX Corp. Earlier, he had a key role in shaping the CME's and future industry's response to the 1987 stock market crash, testifying frequently before Congress on the value and efficacy of the CME's risk management products during volatile market episodes. More recently, President Clinton invited Mr. Sandner to participate in the December 1992 economic summit in Little Rock, where he served as the futures and options industry's sole representative.

Mr. Sandner, formerly a trial attorney, joined the CME in 1971 and has served continuously on its governing board since 1977. He has served on and chaired scores of member committees. In 1978 he became president and CEO of RB&H Inc., a futures commission mer-

chant and clearing member firm of the CME. Jack Sandner has long had a national reputation as a futures trader.

****

Q: *What was it that first attracted you to trading, Jack?*

JACK: Well, I think it was the instantaneous evaluation of my analysis. My personality is such, I like to know the outcome right away. It's almost non-Oriental. I like to know the result of whatever analysis I put forth on a legal issue, or on any kind of issue. In trading, the outcome is immediate. I don't think there is any kind of a model that creates that kind of evaluation that quickly. It allows you to then re-evaluate your decision-making process and that excited me, notwithstanding the fact that it is an opportunity to make some money if you're good at it.

Q: *What's been very interesting to us is we have found in our interviews of the top commodity traders, many of whom you know, that money tended not to be the main reason that they went into trading. This is quite different from the reasons most people choose to trade. So based on your personal experience as a trader and in terms of operating the clearing firm and mentoring and monitoring other traders, how important do you think motive is ultimately to becoming a successful trader?*

JACK: I think motive is all important in anything that you do, because that's what creates the incentives to develop the skills to do it. The skills are not easy to develop, because it requires an emotional set of skills, a mechanical set of skills, and a cerebral set of skills. It requires many, many skills and it takes years to develop all of those skills effectively.

Q: *Could you elaborate?*

JACK: Well, I do want to mention one other thing and that is the issue of money. A lot of traders that you visited with told you that money wasn't the real primary centerpiece of their agenda in trading, and although it's hard to separate money away from it, it makes sense. And I would like to say that I have given a lot of thought to this issue over the years.

When you take someone who is a superior gymnast, he's not in it for the money and yet he spends countless hours disciplining his psychic and his physical ability and everything else. You see that with a lot of sports like Lacrosse. In many sports there's no money in it and so why do people do it? The answer is simple. There's something in it that excites them. Perhaps like with me they're evaluated on results very, very quickly. I think it isn't a perfect on-all-fours analogy, but when I was attracted to trading, I didn't say to myself distinctly "this is like the sport of boxing or gymnastics" (Jack was a champion Golden Gloves boxer), but I had the same feeling, the same surge of adrenaline, the same feeling of excitement of being involved. It is a competitive challenge and the results are whether you are right or wrong. In gymnastics the result is you get a 9.9. Okay, here the result is if you are successful it equates into some kind of a value in terms of monetary value.

It's the atmosphere and the challenge and I don't want to say that trading is a sport, but it has the same kind of model. That is why people go into it not necessarily for the money. It is just the end result for some.

It's hard to distinguish those two things, but I do distinguish between them. There are a lot of other ways to make money, I believe, and some people would rather do it this way, and I was one of them because I enjoyed the sport, so to speak, and the competitive challenge.

I think there is another ingredient here and that is you are evaluated continually. The market is the king and the market and the price evaluates your decision-making process. No matter how you rationalize it, the bottom line is the bottom line. Then you can constantly revisit your analysis whether you are good at it or bad at it. Rather than sojourn years to figure out whether or not your decision-making process is good; in a lot of professions you just never really know.

Q: *Was there a defining moment for you. A moment of epiphany when you realized trading was it for you?*

JACK: No, I don't believe there was one moment. There were moments where I would go the other way. I would say this isn't for me. You're writing a book about traders, but I think my career is a little bit different than most traders, okay? Although I still trade, I've left the trading arena as I knew it for many, many years, quite a few years ago. So I would say that trading for me changed considerably in terms of the psychic income.

Q: *What do you think it takes to become a successful trader? You spoke before about some specific skills . . .*

JACK: Discipline. I could elaborate on what that means; it means different things to different people. But I think one of the main ingredients is focus. They say traders have a nice life. They come in at 8:30 or whatever, and they're gone at 1:00. You see their expensive cars going down the expressway. What people don't realize is that a lot happens before the bell rings and a lot happens after the bell rings.

The other thing people don't realize is between the opening and closing bell a tremendous energy is expended in focus, if you're any good at what you do. I don't know one trader that's any good that doesn't really focus 1,000 percent every second on what he's doing, and is consumed by it. And the traders that aren't good, they sojourn. They're lazy and they'll make money sometimes, but they'll get caught. I think it takes a tremendous attention span and focus of attention on exactly what you're doing. If you don't do that, then the discipline can't follow. You can't be disciplined unless you focus, because it's too easy to look away and rationalize.

Q: *Why is that?*

JACK: Very often people do that because they instinctively or emotionally are unable to face the discipline feature of trading—taking losses or adding to a position. It's very easy to take profits if you're not disciplined, when in actuality you shouldn't be taking profits. You should be adding to the position, knowing that the chances are when you add to that position, the market could step back on you and you will have given up profit. But knowing that the one time that it continues to go in your favor, you'll have a bonanza. A lot of people take profits much too soon, and of course it takes discipline not to. It's very easy to take a profit. It takes a lot of discipline not to.

Q: *How do you get that discipline?*

JACK: You have to constantly focus and pay attention to exactly what you're doing, what your program is, and focus on it. And then the discipline will follow. If you don't focus on it, it's too easy to say I'll take the profit—I'm going to go for lunch.

Q: *In your experience how do you develop that focus?*

JACK: It can be developed in a lot of ways. You can almost instinctively have it, but most traders don't. Or you can associate yourself with positive traders that inevitably will have it and model yourself after them. Someone could be your mentor, telling you when you are showing good focus and when it's obvious you don't have the appropriate focus. But we must remember we're creatures that are flexible and adaptable, we're human beings. And the fittest survive. One out of ten, one out of eight, one out of six or whatever, will develop that focus. And how he does it or she does it, happens in different ways. By example of others, by your own intuition because of life experiences, when you've been successful. Perhaps you focused in sports and were successful, and you were unsuccessful when you didn't. You were successful when you focused in school and you were unsuccessful when you didn't.

But I think generally in behavioral psychology, they would tell you that in order to learn to do anything, you have to at some time have been positively conditioned to the right way and negatively conditioned to the wrong way. So I would suggest that people that learn how to sharpen their trading focus have learned it somewhere else in their life experience and have been reinforced when they have focused, and have been electrically shocked when they haven't. I believe traders learn like a rat in a Skinner box in behavioral conditioning. That's the person that comes in and he's able to focus, he's learned it from life experience.

Now you take someone that didn't have those experiences to learn how to focus, how do they learn it? It's a little harder for them to learn it, so they have to be patient enough to look at people who are successful.

It's almost like shopping for a house in a neighborhood. Do you just say I like that house, and here's the price the real estate person tells me? Or do you do your homework and look at the comparables in that area for the last three years and do your analysis? The person that doesn't instinctively or through life experience have the capability to focus and realize that he should focus doesn't know what he's supposed to be doing or understand the concept of comparables. He doesn't ask himself who's successful and who isn't? Or he isn't patient enough to watch how they do it and try to talk to them and embrace their personality and then try to follow what they are doing that works.

One word of caution. I think life experience in learning to do things is the most convincing way to follow up any course of conduct. I think you're less likely to do it if you say I'm going to model what a successful person does. Not that modeling doesn't work, it does, but it is more difficult because different circumstances present themselves and then you have to go back on your life experience very quickly because you have to make instantaneous decisions, very quick decisions. And you're less likely to make the right decision if you're just sort of trying to mimic somebody, because you don't really know what they would have done in that situation. I mean this specifically in trading with respect to discipline and focus. But if you've had your own life experiences, it's much easier. I think general life experiences add a lot to one's chances of becoming successful at trading.

Q: You touched upon some of the psychological barriers to becoming a successful trader. Not being disciplined, lacking self-confidence, not being focused. What do you think are some of the other psychological barriers which prevent people from being as successful as they could be in trading futures markets?

JACK: Ego. Ego plays a big part in it. The idea that you have to be a winner all the time. And that winning is defined in a very contracted way, rather than a protracted way. You take that ingredient, that you have a huge ego, which means you want to be successful and you want your peers to think you're successful, coupled with a contracted definition of what winning means, like every day I gotta make money. Or the worst would be every trade I have to make money; rather than to say at the end of the month I want to take a look at this, and no matter how many days I lost, if at the end of the month I've made money, then I'm a winner. If you take that protracted look at it, you can deal with it much more easily.

So a big ego, getting involved with it in terms of your own self-worth rather than just being a motivated trader to be a winner over a protracted period of time.

A big ego with a contracted viewpoint of what winning means, I think is a sure formula for disaster! Just total disaster! Because you can't be measured, success can't be measured in this marketplace on your daily activity, whether you made money today or lost money today.

I think every successful trader, if you go back and look at their P&Ss, you'll see, that they had many, many losing days and they end up a big winner. I think if you did a psychological autopsy, and you could get data, you would see that it didn't emotionally strike them in any negative way whatsoever that they lost money during that day! On the other hand, if you took a losing trader and did that same autopsy, I think you'd see that there was a tremendous pulse rate and blood pressure rate when they lost on an individual day. If you could do this on an empirical basis, a scientific basis, then you could say that that would be the progenitor of a losing trader.

Q: What you are saying, Jack, is enormously interesting. You look at people who lose regularly in the markets and they tend to associate losing with their own self-worth. They associate losing with being a loser. The successful traders on the other hand represent their experience much differently. In terms of your own personal trading experience, what was the most difficult psychological barrier for you to overcome?

JACK: I think the whole issue is the ego, you know, wanting to be a winner by a short definition. That's why I feel very comfortable talking about this. Learning to be able to walk out at the end of the day, not having a winning day, and not feeling it affected me emotionally.

Q: *Did you evolve into having that ability, or did you . . .*

JACK: Yeah, evolved into it.

Q: *Didn't have it early?*

JACK: No. I had a lot of other things, focus early, from all the sports, but I didn't have that psychological feature of what winning really meant, I had to learn that.

Q: *Can you think of an actual trade that you might have had, or an experience in the market that actually heightened your awareness of the psychological features of trading?*

JACK: Oh, I think averaging. The tendency to average the market, heightened my experience and awareness of the psychology of trading. When you get the numbers on averaging, and what it does to you, and what causes you to average. What causes you to do it is your inability to accept your definition of not winning or losing. Which is to say that if you define a position as this is either a winner or loser, and that's the end result, and that your obsessed with winning, you will tend to average.

But if you define this as a process over a period of time, this isn't a winner or loser, the market is going against me now I turn around, your in a scalping mode rather than in a trend mode and you do it on a more protracted basis, then you don't deal with it that way, and then you don't average because you know that that generally rings a death knell for your trading.

But you'll see most young traders tend to want to average and that's because they define each trade as being a winner or a loser. So if you start to lose, you know if I average that trade and double the position, or however you want to average, that your chances are that it will come back partially, and you'll get your money back four out of five times. But the fifth time it's a disaster! What causes you to do that? It's psychologically possessing the wrong definition of winning and losing. So that is the readjustment and mind set that has to be made for a good trader. That's what I had to learn.

Q: *Through experience?*

JACK: Experience.

Q: *Yes, experience is a great teacher. Speaking of experience, when things are going against you in the market, what is your internal dialogue like, what are you telling yourself? What are you saying in your mind's eye? What are you hearing? What are you feeling?*

JACK: What I am telling myself is that this is temporary and that it's the market and that I am doing all the things right. I am disciplined and focused and that I have to just stay the term, not the position, and it will all come back. Just to relax, be in a good state of mind. I think the worse thing that can happen is when things are going badly that you get real uptight about it and that you overindulge yourself. That takes you a lot longer to work yourself out of.

Q: *So what you're saying is basically, you have to keep yourself upbeat. You can't allow yourself to be in a limited state of mind.*

JACK: You have to have tremendous confidence in your self and your ability, and that trading is a cycle, like everything else is a cycle, and at the end of the term the cycle will turn your way if you have confidence in yourself and do all the right things.

So you have to constantly tell yourself that it's a cycle, an inevitable cycle, and since it's inevitable, it will work its way out. If you don't tell yourself that, and you say that my trading stinks or I'm a disaster, you will get tremendously uptight, such as a basketball player who shoots normally 78 percent of his free throws and all of a sudden, in the play-offs, a player like Scottie

Pippen, who is a very talented guy, starts shooting a much lower percent. Something is happening, and if he just relaxes it's all going to come back to a normal center. That's how it is with trading.

Q: *Now how do you personally do that as a trader? How do you center Jack Sandner? How do you get yourself to that state of mind which allows you to be confident?*

JACK: I always say that this is the first day of the rest of my life, and I come in optimistic with the glass half full, and I'm able, even if that first day of the rest of my life turns out to be negative. I start the next day by telling myself today is the first day of the rest of my life, and I'm going to keep the same physiology and anatomy and gray matter that I had before when I was successful, and I'm going to keep doing the same successful thing. See, I'm very fearful of getting uptight and I think if a Scottie Pippen, for example, gets uptight about missing 7 out of 10 free throws, he'll miss 7 out of 10 again. So he's just got to constantly look at each individual thing. Each individual free throw is a relaxed situation and bring his talents to bear on that. Now of course, this is assuming that you are competent in terms of your methodology to begin with. It's assuming that it is Scottie Pippen and not somebody that doesn't shoot baskets. So you've got to assume that there is a premise there that you are successful or committed to begin with.

Q: *It comes from confidence?*

JACK: Yeah.

Q: *You can't be overconfident if that talent doesn't exist? If you're not competent?*

JACK: Right.

Q: *When things are really going well for you, what are you telling yourself? What are you seeing? What do you hear?*

JACK: I just feel good. You know, I'm telling myself just stay in sync.

Q: *Some of the traders that we spoke to said that there were particular images that come to mind. Is there any particular image or the voice of someone that keeps you calm when things are going against you?*

JACK: No, not really. I can't think of anything. You know, you just try to feel good, like you're centered; you try to stay in sync and in rhythm with everything.

Q: *You mentioned being positive and constantly seeing that glass as half full and wanting to keep that same physiology. So really, what your offering to people who are looking at how to maintain that strong feeling, is that you personally look to have that same feeling of confidence even when things are going against you so you can keep your focus clear and strong?*

JACK: Right. Absolutely.

Q: *It's a little harder though when things . . .*

JACK: It's harder; that's the difference between success and failure. Like I said before you've got to have a protracted view of things and confidence in yourself. You've got to have a lot of self-esteem. If you come in to this marketplace having been an abused child with no self-esteem, it's going to be very, very hard. You've got to have a lot of confidence, so I don't know if there's a formula that would say if you don't have self-esteem you can't make it. Intuition tells me that you have to have a lot of confidence and self-esteem to become a successful trader.

Q: *That has definitely been true of our experience interviewing traders. They point out that self-esteem is key. We're not clear though,* *whether or not people are born with this, whether it comes from background, or it's something that they've gained, just as a result of being successful at trading. In other words, perhaps it just builds upon itself. I was wondering, in your case, if it's something that came out of your participation in sports?*

JACK: I think people who have suffered adversity and have overcome adversity many many times are able to become good traders. In my life, I have had a lot of adversity and overcame it. So I have been positively conditioned by doing certain things. I find a way to overcome adversity. So, for me, trading wasn't that difficult of a discipline to learn because trading is full of adversity, and so how do you overcome it? How do you stay with the program and press on? I think when you grow up and have a lot of life experience with adversity and learn ways to overcome them you are confident that no matter how bad the situation is you tell yourself, "I can survive." I can think of countless times in trading where things were adverse, but if I didn't have the right attitude, I would have crumbled and walked away and never have been able to come back.

Q: *Jack, could you give us a specific example?*

JACK: Well, there was one book written about the cattle situation I got involved in when the DES scare hit the market. At the same time the Hunt fiasco happened and I was really getting destroyed. I could have just blown myself away in the market with that horrible adversity, but through it all I felt confident that if I could just see it through that I would be able to get back on my feet. It was very difficult but I did it. I was just elected the chairman of the Exchange for the first time in 1980, and rather young for that position. It added a lot of pressure because I was chairman and getting nailed in the market. It was March 27, 1980; and I was just seeing it through. There were other trading situations that I got caught in. You've been in it in its ups and downs. How do you deal with it? You have to come back, you start small again and always say that there's another window to climb through.

It's an interesting issue because now we have kids that grow up that have never suffered rejection. And parents, because of their affluence and their love, are able to manipulate the environment where the children never fail. I think these people have a tremendous problem learning how to trade. They never experience a valley of tears. If you have never suffered adversity you are going to have a real difficult time dealing with it for the first time as a trader. We all must experience it. If you are unprepared you will never know how.

Q: *I think that metaphor works very well for trading because there are a lot of tears and you've got to develop the ability to be resilient.*

JACK: I discourage people from trading if I love them. (Jack laughs.) I do. My kids aren't down here. Because it's very painful for me to see them go through this process. I don't care how good you are, nobody walks in and makes it. One trader who we both know, I don't have all the numbers, but I think he's probably the best of all time. I would hazard a guess that even he has had some very painful moments.

Q: *I could attest to that.*

JACK: Yes, and you were very close to him.

Q: *He will tell you that.*

JACK: When they come to the Merc you know there will be many tears and you hope that they can overcome those tears and there will be many smiles. But how many don't? Look at the people who say, "I want to be a trader," but they don't look at the people that are being carried out of here all the time. Enduring the pain is just part of the process and its like anything else, you just have to put in the hours and you have to feel the muscle aches and you have to feel the frustration.

Q: *There's one commonality that everyone shares and that is all traders, from the very best to those who are still struggling, experience frustration. However, what we're seeing very clearly, and I guess it's something that you've alluded to, is that the difference between the great traders and the unsuccessful traders is that the top traders find ways within themselves to go beyond setbacks to reach their goals. What we found is that personal belief systems are a major factor to determine whether one is successful or not in this business. What are some beliefs that you possess about yourself as a trader which allow you to be successful at what you do?*

JACK: I just believe in myself. I see that I can do just about anything if I put my mind to it. I can't dunk a basketball, but I'll find another way to get the ball in the basket. I believe totally in my abilities. Maybe I'm overambitious in my confidence in what I can do, but I will then accomplish whatever goals I set by believing strongly in myself. I've always had that attitude about myself. I cannot visualize myself looking at the trading floor and taking on the challenge of trading and not winning. I can't imagine it, that's just my attitude. I don't think Joel Greenberg— I think he's a perfect example of a guy who has a tremendous belief in himself. He went through a difficult period and he did it with class and he came back. He had to have a tremendous belief in himself. That he looks at that floor and says, "I can conquer it," and he's right, he can! And so I think I have always had tremendous belief in myself which has allowed me to become successful.

I think there is one other thing that needs to be said. It's the reverse side of the equation. It's probably the same thing just the mirror image of it. If you have this tremendous fear of failing—

you've got to have a reasonable amount of fear to do well—but if the fear is overwhelming, you won't do well. You will do things that are unnatural and then you will fail. So you have to have balance. It's just like going into a boxing ring, and you're so afraid of losing or getting knocked out that you run all the time. You're going to lose! But if you have enough fear to make you perform well, then that fear is good fear, but you can't allow yourself to be controlled by that fear.

Q: *It's like you said earlier, Jack, where you spoke about the importance of focus. If you focus on fear, you are going to get fear. If your focus is dominated by failure, it is only natural you're going to get failure. If your focus is on success, however you define it, and if you have the methodology to get you there, you just have to succeed at trading and anything else.*

JACK: Absolutely. Focus is the key.

Q: *You spoke before about modeling behaviors, you spoke about mentors. I was wondering how important was it for you to have a mentor or a role model?*

JACK: You see, I didn't. It would have been nice if I did. It would have been a lot easier for me. But I just had to learn for myself.

I think with my life experience, if I had a role model immediately, I would have been a lot better off. But I didn't have that. I really wasn't born into this industry where people had money, descendants, and friends from school to guide you. I knew virtually no one when I came here. I was a lawyer, and I didn't even know who to model myself after!

God help me if I would have modeled myself after the wrong traders.

You know when you are analyzing what it takes to be a successful trader, sometimes it's very helpful to look at the disasters in order to learn what occurred and to analyze and learn from their experience.

Q: *Yes, that's definitely true as we both know there are traders who had a great deal of talent and they did have confidence and they did at times have focus but they couldn't make it. Why is that? What separated these traders from the people who are able to make it time and time again to the finish line?*

JACK: That fear of losing and greed. If you look at those guys, the ones that I mentioned, their focus wasn't absolutely there. They felt some comfort, and maybe an edge in the deck which is bullshit as far as I'm concerned, it's an illusion. All those things distract you away from having focus, and it's focus that gives you discipline and self-confidence and, ultimately, success.

Q: *Now you mentioned that you didn't have a specific mentor in the industry, but I'm wondering if there is someone who you can point to in your background as a mentor who gave you certain qualities of character or conviction which you were able to apply to trading.*

JACK: Well, in boxing there was Tony Zale. I mean there are people that you look at in life that you respect. Fred Lane the trial attorney, he has a tremendous stoic attitude. I've always revered Fred Lane.

Tony Zale always had a tremendous discipline and focus and he was the middleweight champion of the world. And Fred Lane is one of the best trial attorneys in the world, and is able to accept the ups and the downs when witnesses turn on him and what have you. So these two people were real character models for me.

In this industry Leo Melamed provided a great leadership example for me. As for trading, I would have loved to have gotten into George Segal's mind and found out what makes him tick . . . also Ralph Peters.

Q: *What words of advice would you have for someone who is deeply committed to becoming a successful trader?*

JACK: Well I think you have to do a self-evaluation of whether or not you have the personality profile to be a trader or the potential personality profile to be a trader. In order to do that you have to define what is a good trader. You have to have some kind of evidence of what makes a good trader so that you can compare. I mean people do all sorts of psychological testing now that's pretty reliable and available, but it has to be compared to something. Whether you're suitable for this profession or that profession it happens all over the place. It's a big industry as a matter of fact.

So for example you shouldn't think about playing basketball if you're going to be under five foot seven. Okay, you just shouldn't, it would be nice to think about it but choose another career. So that's easy, but this is very hard because it takes two things. First, what is the profile that makes a successful career? I know you're going to try to address that in your book and second of all, how do you evaluate whether you fit into that profile? I think that's an introspective evaluation.

Q: *What would you say that that profile is?*

JACK: I think that we've talked a lot about it. The ability to focus, confidence, discipline, and life experience to accept adversity. How are you emotionally at working out problems and are you able to do it. Did your mother die? How did you handle that? Things like that. Whatever those life experiences are.

Q: *It's interesting that you mention that. I just want to say something about that. I lost my mother when I was fairly young.*

JACK: How did you handle your mother dying? What did you learn from that? Your pain is less today than it was the day of her death.

Q: *Exactly.*

JACK: And you need time and if you stay with it . . .

Q: *I think you learn, you learn that you can endure. Which I think is something that you were talking about, you're feelings of overcoming adversity, and as you talked about Tony Zale and Fred Lane . . . I mean these are people who were survivors.*

JACK: Yes . . . for example, and I don't know if anyone has mentioned this, we have known of a few suicides down here over the years. I think that I can make an argument that the propensity to commit suicide was a personality flaw, a personality characteristic, whether it was chemical depression, whatever it was, the person had a proclivity toward a sense of hopelessness and despair and not being able to work things out. Someone would say that he committed suicide because he lost at trading. I would say that his tendency toward being suicidal preceded his becoming a trader.

Actually his losses in the market and his failure at trading were almost predetermined by his propensity to fall into a state of hopelessness where he has no self-esteem and no confidence. Those personality characteristics—see, if I could have defined the personality profile . . . if you brought me a depressive person I would say don't trade. Because you can't be a depressive person, and be a good trader. That would be my analysis.

When you try to say what it takes to make a successful trader, someone is going to say okay that's what it takes and I'm going to learn to do that. But there is a corollary to that. If you don't have those things, you'll be unsuccessful and certain people shouldn't enter this, just like a kid five foot five shouldn't hang his hat on being a professional basketball player. So if you can define these things you just don't go into those occupations.

Q: *What we're finding—and it's confirmed with almost every conversation that we've had and once again with you—it seems to us that someone like you, if I'm not being too presumptuous in saying this, a guy like you can't fail. And successful traders can't fail because even when things aren't working out for them they never view it as failure. They don't represent it to themselves as failure.*

JACK: My self-esteem, I don't think it was ever lowered by one iota even though I took some tremendous, some might say staggering losses in the market. I always felt good about myself. Maybe I'd have to go and jerry-rig it a little bit and go out and run five miles and by the third mile I'd say, hey I'm ready to conquer the world again. But I always had a way of surviving and working it out. I refused to see myself as a failure.

Some people drink. Which means, yeah that will work for a short period of time and then you become an alcoholic and you're destroyed. Some people take cocaine, who knows! Whatever! Everybody is looking for a way out of that pain. It's the people that know the healthy way out of the pain and how to turn it into a healthy experience. And what gives you that ability to do that? Positive life experience. Overcoming adversity and disciplining yourself. The best way is positive life experience.

Q: *What you're saying then is using difficult life experience or trading experiences in order to achieve self-trust and confidence.*

JACK: That's what I'm talking about. The ability to have had adversity and overcome it to stay positive and strong and confident.

Chapter Thirteen

Jeffrey L. Silverman

Jeffrey L. Silverman is an independent trader and member of the Chicago Mercantile Exchange. He has twenty-five years experience as a position trader of futures, options, and cash commodities with extensive experience trading a broad range of financial and physical derivatives.

In addition, he has been an active participant in exchange governance, serving as chairman of the following committees: Managed Funds and Derivatives, Joint Marketing Subcommittee of the Financial Oversight and Agricultural Oversight Committees, New Products (physical commodities), and Agricultural Options.

He holds a Bachelor of Science degree from Massachusetts Institute of Technology with a concentration in economics and finance. While at MIT he studied with Paul Samuelson and Paul Cootner ("random walk" theorist). He was associated with Commodities Corp. in its formative stages.

Mr. Silverman describes himself as an active student of the philosophy, psychology, and general theory of markets.

****

Q: *Why did you start to trade?*

JEFFREY: I was about thirteen years old. . . . From an early age I was a very driven individual. At that age, I was trying to figure out what I wanted to do with my life. I was plowing through the library at my middle school. I was in junior high, in Omaha, Nebraska. I was reading autobiographies. You know, you had the Dewey Decimal System and they are all in one place. I forget what number but anyway I came across a biography of Bernard Baruch and I decided that for a kid from Omaha, Jewish, growing up in an age when banking and commerce were, for the most part, excluded . . . you could be a professional. You could be a stockbroker. But I was attracted to the career of Bernard Baruch. Being a financier and arbitrageur sounded extremely fascinating and far away from the prosaic life I knew growing up in Omaha, Nebraska.

Q: *Would you say, then, it was a fascination with a lifestyle?*

JEFFREY: No, I wouldn't say that at all. It was well before I had any concept that there was a lifestyle that could be associated with trading. There were discussions of Baruch's private train and his hunting estate, but more than anything else, I think it boiled down to a recognition on my part at a very early age that I wanted to be compensated based solely on what I did, not on how people appraised me. I was cognizant of the fact that my handwriting suffered, and as a result of my handwriting being poor, I got graded down relative to my peers in school. I resented the power that my teachers held over my life in the form of awards and punishments or grades. I vowed that if I was ever able to pick an occupation, the occupation would not have as a criteria the judgment of other people about how good a job I did!

Q: *So what you really wanted was independence?*

JEFFREY: Effectively yes, I had to get paid totally based on how well I did, not how some boss or some teacher evaluated my performance. Independence in the sense I wanted compensation for performance based solely on some objective standard. In the marketplace you get paid for performance and it's a ruthlessly objective standard. You're either right or you're wrong and they reward you for good performance plain and simple. It gets right down to the nitty gritty.

Q: *It's certainly hard to argue with that. In your opinion, what does it take to become a successful trader?*

JEFFREY: Well, before you can answer that question, I think you need to ask yourself, what is the game of trading all about? A professor of finance, Paul Cootner, obviously has given this whole subject a lot of thought, and I think it's right down the alley that you're going with this. By the way, Cootner is known for editing the book, *The Random Walk Character of Stock Market Prices.* The sole idea of the book is that stock prices are random. Of course markets look random, but it doesn't mean that they necessarily are random!

Paul said to me once that commodity futures trading is a zero sum game which exists for the sheer purpose of transfer-ring wealth from the hyphenated word "dumber-players" to the hyphenated word "smarter-players." This gets in right to the subject of *The Innergame of Trading.* It's not raw intelligence. It's being able to apply that intelligence as a player. A player in the sense of a poker game. A player in the sense of the Robert Altman movie, "The Player." It's all those definitions of being a player in life that are crucial. So, you can have someone who's absolutely a zero in intelligence, but is a consummate player and makes a lot of money in this game based on his psychology and how he plays the game.

Q: *If you had to identify specific psychological traits of successful traders such as yourself, what are they?*

JEFFREY: I can't really speak for other successful traders. As far as myself, it's an incredible willingness and commitment to study and to search for what works pragmatically, not necessarily what is theoretically correct. It is an ability to throw theory aside and say I want to figure out what works. I'll figure out why it works later, but I'm looking for tools that will enable me to forecast the market. That will enable me to forecast the direction. Will enable me to forecast major timing turns better than anybody else. If I can do those things, I'll get paid, but I'm not trying to forecast price levels. I'm trying to forecast something that's working, always with a focus on making money. Being right the market, not on being right the fundamentals, not on being right anything else, but being right the market. Focus, dedication, just being willing to do whatever it takes to win at the game.

Q: *What do you think are the psychological barriers for most traders?*

JEFFREY: It's a very interesting thing. The primary psychological barriers are two. One, lack of discipline and two, inflexibility. Inflexibility, inability to recognize when the market's turned. Typically, a person gets in a position, they develop a disciplined trading style where they're going to sit with that position through thick and thin, waiting for it to grow to fruition.

I'm talking as a long-term position trader where I have gravitated, where it seems to me that the serious money is made. That very discipline of sticking to a position at some point creates the situation where you can put your head in the sand and ignore the negative evidence in your position. What I'm also saying is you have to have the flexibility, while your sticking and staying, to turn around and look at it and say, gee, I may be wrong here and then get out! That flexibility not to go down on sinking ships separates the winners from the losers. It's a discipline to have a plan. Be unemotional about getting in.

Be unemotional about the position and be unemotional about getting out.

Q: *It seems the ability to overcome our natural emotions is one of the more difficult aspects of trading.*

JEFFREY: Well, that's where all the discipline comes in. Doing things that avoid having an emotional content in your decision making.

Q: *Any other things you can think of that would prevent somebody psychologically from being able to be successful at trading?*

JEFFREY: I think one of the hardest things for me to learn was that the margin requirements are only related to the amount that the market's going to move in a day. To be really successful at trading, you have to develop a disciplined money management program that's going to enable you to separate, as the electrical engineers would call it, the signal from the noise. You can get very good at defining what the signal is and what the major trend is, but unless you discipline yourself with an effective technique the noise will get you. You're going to end up losing money, irrespective of how good you are at defining the signal. The markets will kill you if you don't avoid swinging for the fences all the time. I can't tell you how many years it took me to learn that.

Q: *Are you saying you have to swing for the fences all of the time?*

JEFFREY: No, you have to avoid swinging for the fences. The only way you can make any serious money is by not swinging for the fences. If you're constantly swinging for the fences the noise is going to get you.

Q: *But you said a moment ago that you learned that it's the long-term trader who makes the serious money.*

JEFFREY: Well, to me, not swinging for the fences is really a measure of how leveraged you are. If you're using a margin-to-equity ratio that is more than one for five, you're swinging for the fences and you're going to strike out.

Q: *You're relating it to margined equity. How about percentage gains to equity?*

JEFFREY: I look at what I think the risk is in a position. I look at what I think the return is likely to be. I try and maximize what's in my account in terms of the most bang for the buck. In terms of return for risk. In terms of return for margin dollar investment. Then, as I've gotten more successful, I tend to just keep dialing down the amount of risk per margin dollar so that I can trade with an even longer term perspective.

Q: *To keep the noise from interfering with the game plan, the signal, you reduce the amount of leverage you might use so that you don't have to worry about the noise as much, is that basically what you said?*

JEFFREY: Yeah. Then, there was one other thing. Among the things I do is I collect quotes from the gurus of the business. I'm reminded of a quote that I heard from Monty Monaster. He is kind of a legend in this business. He's about 75 years old, been trading commodities for zillions of years. He said once, "The young guys today, they have all the time in the world and no patience. I have all the patience in the world and no time." What I've attempted to learn from that dictum, utilizing the sense that you're only going to make money if you can trade the long-term signal, is that you must ignore the noise and be real patient. Something else along those lines came out when they asked Bernard Baruch the secret to his success, his answer was, "I always sold too soon."

So you get into the what does he mean by that. You sell it before the top. You sell it when everybody wants to buy it.

Baruch didn't get the maximum dollar on every trade, but he sold it before the risk/reward probably went to hell on his trades. I just think there's lots of very interesting strategies to be garnered from an intensive study of the sayings of the old masters. I've gone out and collected them and thought about them and instilled them and tried to utilize them in the way I conduct my business.

Q: *What was your most challenging psychological barrier to overcome as a trader?*

JEFFREY: Just giving up the desire to fully utilize the margin of my trading account.

Q: *Moving from a short-term to a long-term trader?*

JEFFREY: Well, I was always a long-term trader, but by giving up this deathwish to overtrade, I was able to focus more on the long-term signal and less on the noise, I was able to trade in the market and buy it when it was value and sell it when it was not.

Q: *Do you see yourself as a fundamentalist or a technician?*

JEFFREY: Fundamentalist.

Q: *So, you basically look to the fundamentals of a market and take a long-term view and attempt to determine market direction?*

JEFFREY: Yeah, I try to beat the other players at the game by having more patience and a bigger bank roll behind me. The poker analogy is an interesting one. When thinking about the Cootner statement about the zero sum game, shifting wealth from the dumber players to the smarter players.

I envision the world as a trading world, as a giant casino, if you will, with a bunch of tables for poker. I long ago decided that if I'm going to have to play this game and I want to win at this game, I want to sit down at the table where I'm, one, the smartest player, and two, I have every possible legal advantage available to me, and three, where I've got a longer-term, more patient attitude than any of the other players, and four, where I've got a bigger bank roll. Then, if I play long enough and I have enough edges, I will have all the chips.

Archemedes said, "Give me a lever long enough and a place to stand and I'll move the earth." Commodity trading is essentially a highly leveraged game and leverage can cut both ways. Unless you increase the signal to a noise ratio of your trading and reduce the noise portion to your equity, you're going to be a loser.

Q: *What about the fear of losing? You know how most traders focus on watching their equity rather than the market. It's just a psychological barrier they can't seem to overcome.*

JEFFREY: I think what you're getting down to is that when you're focusing on the noise, fear and greed come in. Fear in particular, if you're overtrading. Greed comes in because when you've got the market going your way, you have a tendency toward increasing the size of the position to the limits of your money. But if you follow a disciplined system and keep the margined equity ratio low or the equity margin ratio high, you avoid those emotions. I think it's fear and greed and hope that are the enemies of futures traders. You have to do a lot of mechanical things before you ever decide to trade, or decide to make a trade that will get control of all those things. So, I don't mention them, but they're certainly extreme barriers. Surprisingly enough, the simplest things that work go back to the first things that people ever told me about trading.

Q: *What did they tell you?*

JEFFREY: To deal with this whole question of money management. Then, you don't have to deal with fear and greed because your trading is disciplined and unemotional. This brings me to another issue: superstition. When I was swinging more for the fences, I used to have this theory that when I felt so good about the market that I'd listen to the radio, I thought listening to the radio made the market go against me. What I failed to recognize, until I spent five years in therapy, is that listening to the radio was a statement that my mind was becoming so supremely overconfident that everybody else in the same position was equally overconfident and everybody in the opposite position was throwing in the towel, that that was the moment to get out!

Invariably within a day or two of my deciding to listen to the radio on the way to or from work, I'd get creamed. There was a similar indication of when you were overtrading or overstaying a market and that was when you started looking at cars. I'm the only person in this whole world who owns a $100,000 Toyota or owned a $100,000 Toyota or a $1,000,000 Ferarri and we're not talking that they cost a million. It cost me $1,000,000!!! I quickly learned that the first sign of expansive thinking for me was when I started thinking about buying a car or vacation home. It was a clear indication that instead of reaching up to pat yourself on the back for being so smart, you should be reaching for the phone and telling your broker to get you out.

Q: *Euphoric trading! What about when things are going against you in the marketplace, what do you tell yourself? Specifically, what do you visualize in your mind, what are you hearing or saying to yourself, what do you feel at these times?*

JEFFREY: I go back to the basics and evaluate what I'm doing wrong and what I'm missing and try and get at the truth. Has there been a fundamental change in the way the market works? Has there been a fundamental change that I'm not aware of?

Q: *Do you ever focus on the money that is changing day to day?*

JEFFREY: That's a disastrous trap. Of course I "look" at the money, but it's a disastrous trap to focus on it because the market doesn't care whether you're long or short or how much you're making or losing. Your goal is to make money and be like the market. Anything that detracts from that is something that's getting in your way and blurring your focus.

Q: *When you are not focusing do you start beating yourself up psychologically?*

JEFFREY: No, if I've decided that it's reached my loss point, I get the hell out and evaluate it later and I'll figure out what I missed later and learn from my mistakes which brings me to a whole other paradigm. I remember some years ago, sitting down with my father-in-law and telling him that I went through life making all the mistakes one could make. As I got better, I'd make the same mistakes fewer times before I'd learn the painful lesson. Then, I got smart. I started learning from the mistakes of others.

It was much cheaper than learning from my own mistakes. I became self-confident as a result of that. My father-in-law said to me, "Dummy, why do you worry about mistakes so much? Just look around and see who's doing the smartest thing and follow what he does." I'd been doing that in a small degree and less intensely, but I was more focused on mistakes in the early part of my career then in the later part of my career, I've been more focused lately on figuring out the way the smart people are doing it. They don't tell you how they're doing it. I figure out how they're doing it and try to emulate the behavior of the smartest.

Q: *Can you give me an example of an important mistake that you learned from early in your career?*

JEFFREY: Yeah, I remember it clearly. It was a mistake I learned from someone else. Probably the first one that got me thinking about my own mistakes and learning from someone else's mistakes.

I put on this significant trade, long cattle, in the early part of 1983. I was short hogs against it because I thought the only thing that could hurt the long cattle position is if there was suddenly a surprise that there were a whole lot of hogs. I did the spread near even money and it got to $.10. Another trader we know had loaded up with the same thing.

He was chartering a plane to go to the Louisville basketball game, Final Four. So he's got this solid enough position that he gets out at $.10 or $.11, and by the time he comes back it's $.125. Then he starts selling it short because he wants to get it back cheaper than he got out and the thing runs to $.22 and ends up getting out at $.20. A 10-cents loss on the cattle and hog spread, this is a lot of money on a big position.

I learned that you've got to get out for a rational reason, not just to get out. Then, once having gotten out, I learned that just because I sold it, it's not necessarily going to go down. Why fight the market? So, there's a lot of lessons to be learned.

Q: *When things are really going well for you in the market, like this cattle-hog spread you spoke about or you have a series of good winners, what are you saying to yourself then, what are you hearing, seeing, feeling about yourself?*

JEFFREY: I try to get more inner-focused on whether or not the tell-tale signs of expansiveness are creeping into my thinking— whether or not the people on the opposite side are getting ready to throw in the towel. That's the moment that you've got to absolutely turn around the position and take the money.

Many other people collect these little sayings. Like Charlie McVane said, "When the ducks are quacking, you have to feed them." That's a very interesting saying and if you can imagine the ducks visually and they are screaming and quacking and they're biting you at your pant legs—when everybody's screaming that they've got to have the position that you have on, you've got to think of them as a bunch of ducks that want to be fed. Until you feed the ducks, you haven't made any money. Bruce Johnson put the same thing a different way and he said, "When the circus is in town, you've got to sell peanuts." Now, that puts it in even a better perspective because the circus isn't going to be here forever. When they want the peanuts, you better sell them to them. I guess if you don't feed the ducks, somebody else will feed the ducks and they'll walk away when they're full. Though, I've never seen ducks walk away, but if you throw enough food at them, I imagine they will walk away too.

Q: *It seems to me that psychologically you really have overcome your emotional side.*

JEFFREY: Yeah, I can say that categorically, I want to avoid emotion, which is not to say that it's all scientific. I think there's science and art.

Q: *There's a feel to the market. I assume that's what you mean.*

JEFFREY: I'm really saying that there is science and there is art and there's something in art that I can't quantify and I call it "feel." Maybe your definition of feel and my definition of feel— you know, people say the market looks great, it's really acting well. Maybe that's their idea of "feel." My idea of art is something different than what most people would call "feel."

Q: *What is your idea?*

JEFFREY: Some sorts of settled forms of analysis that are beyond scientific comprehension and enable you to pick markets to trade with, places to buy and sell them. Markets where you can't really come up with a quantifiable, scientific, fundamental reason why you're doing something. It's all involved in being a player as opposed to being merely intelligent. It's art rather than science. What I'm really trying to say is success in futures trading is not all science. It's not all intellect. It's part intellect and part art.

There's another really interesting thing; trying to have patience in the market. It is really difficult because you have a 24-hour day and you're focused and intense. Someone like I am, it's really hard to be focused and intent on the market for 24 hours without getting emotionally involved and/or depressed and go through all these mood swings. A lot of traders get involved with traveling and various other things that they do to take their mind off what their positions are and do something else to get busy. Lately, I've gotten heavily involved in exchange governance activities and to some people it's distracting to a fault to have a lot of things going on.

I find that if I've got five areas that I'm working on, that I can have a problem that's intractable in one area and can go on to a success in other areas. While I'm doing something else, then I come back to the insoluble problem and somehow the subconscious has worked through the intractable problem. Getting away from being focused full time on markets, I find greatly diminishes my mood swings.

It's been said that the human mind only uses some minuscule portion of its capability. I assume that's because there's only so much that can fit into the conscious area and most people don't have a way of tapping into the unconscious and turning that into a part of the computer that works. I found recently by having a number of other activities to keep me busy and by focusing on different things, I don't get so emotionally involved.

Q: *But, if you find yourself, let's say, being expansive as you put it, do you find yourself saying specific things to yourself in order to get you back into a better state of mind? Do you say, "Uh oh, I'm really thinking expansively"? Do you say to yourself, "I better not do this?"*

JEFFREY: I probably would say something to myself like I better not do this and then I'd be sitting there thinking that maybe I should use this as a signal that I need to get out of something. I'd go on a very specific hunt for reasons why I should unload what I have.

Q: *What if you have one or two or a series of trades that don't work out? Do you say anything to yourself then?*

JEFFREY: I just go back to the basics and study harder and try harder and focus more intently on what I'm trying to do. I dial down the leverage and just keep working at it.

Q: *What are some of the beliefs you have of yourself as a trader?*

JEFFREY: I believe in myself. I'm very critical. I always feel I could have done better. I think that's part of the reason why I do so well is because I'm always setting the highest possible standard as the basic standard that I'll accept for myself. I never get close so I probably am more self-critical and harder on myself than anybody can believe.

Q: *Do you believe yourself to be more courageous, smarter?*

JEFFREY: You know, there are old commodity traders and there are bold commodity traders, but there are no old, bold commodity traders. In this world you get paid for providing an economic service. You get paid for sticking your hand in the fire as a trader. You get paid for buying them when everybody wants to sell them and selling them when everyone wants to buy them. Nothing else pays. So, yeah, courageous, but I use that sticking your hand in the fire analogy as, since I'm going to get paid for this, I better make sure I do my homework first.

I better make sure I know where value is. Have all the tools in my arsenal ready for it and stick my hand in the fire. I believe that no matter what size you trade, I think you should trade as if you were trading a 10,000 contract position in terms of let's say the cattle market. That's the whole day's volume. In terms of the open interest of 70,000–80,000, that's a huge position. If you trade like a ten-lot trader, you're zipping in and out, and you don't really have a firm basis in the timing of your trade to when you're sticking your hand, maximally, into the fire. The 10,000 car trader can only buy it when everybody wants to sell. So, strangely enough, that's the timing rule, even if you're trading a 100 lot. You force yourself to buy it when the 10,000 car trader would buy it. Force yourself to sell it when the 10,000 car trader would sell it, which is a lot of what Bernard Baruch said—"I always sold too soon." The only time a 10,000 car trader can sell them is when everybody wants to buy them and the people who are already along with you think it's way too soon to sell them.

Q: *Do you have a role model or mentor that has made a difference for you in your trading?*

JEFFREY: I wouldn't say that I have any one mentor or role model. I went out and aggressively read all the literature about trading. I read all the literature about psychology and markets. I studied the wisdom of the masters and read everything that Warren Buffet wrote about trading and his annual reports for the last 20 years. I worked at this thing. I got paid for doing a lot of hard work.

Q: *You're taking a lot of information from other successful people and doing similar things?*

JEFFREY: Yeah, and I codified their little dictums. I wrote them down, thought about them in terms of what they meant. When I was a kid growing up, my grandfather who had come over, well, both of them, but one of my grandfathers had come over from Russia when he was a teenager with a third- or fourth-grade education. He'd always relate everything in terms of a parable. If you think about the Bible it's all parables. It's basically how language is used to distill observations into important kernels of truth and then passed on. It's your job as the recipient of this kernel of truth to figure out what it all means and apply it. As someone once said "How come I'm too soon old and too late smart?" These kernels of wisdom are out there and you just have to collect them and figure out what they mean and figure out how to utilize them in your trading.

I've sought out a whole lot of role models and successful traders and boiled down from their statements to kernels of practical truth. I've done this very assiduously. I've taken all these statements and put them into kernel form and figured out what they mean and figured out how to apply them. I figured out a number of things on my own from the literature and I've created my own little parables and utilized them in my trading. Somehow my subconscious is programmed with all of these things and at appropriate times, they come to me automatically.

Q: *I'm going to put this question to you and then I'm going to ask you if you need a kernel to answer this question. What words of advice or encouragement would you offer to someone who's committed to becoming a successful trader?*

JEFFREY: I don't have a specific, but I do know you've got to be willing to work hard and know yourself. You must spend the time—you must study the characteristics of successful traders. You must study your own mistakes. You must study the mistakes of the others around you. Increasing levels of sophistication will put you in the direction of understanding who you are. You must really study your own self and understand what you're all about. It's not clear to me whether I didn't do this whole thing backwards where I studied the economics and science of trading and worked into the psychology of trading and finally got involved in some sort of philosophical thinking of the whole trading process. It's not clear to me that I didn't do the whole thing backwards and shouldn't have studied philosophy and psychology at the start and it might have made the whole process easier.

Q: *I have thought about that and I wonder if doing it backwards, as you say, is the natural progression for a successful trader such as yourself.*

JEFFREY: The only reason I mentioned that is because among a few traders that I know that are highly successful, I can think of Joe Richey at CRT and Richard Dennis and Charlie McVane, all highly successful traders. All had bachelor's degrees in philosophy, which prepared them for absolutely nothing, other than thinking. When I asked this one guy on the floor, "What does Charlie say about his degree in philosophy?" His quote from Charlie, was "Philosophy teaches me to ask the right question. It gives me the ability to separate the truth from the bullshit."

Chapter Fourteen

Bruce Johnson

Bruce Johnson began his association with the futures market in 1965 when he was a chalkboard marker at the old Mercantile Exchange. In 1969, after completing law school, he became a principal of Packers Trading Co., a futures commission merchant. Mr. Johnson is widely regarded as an expert and player in the livestock markets.

****

Q: *What first attracted you to trading?*

BRUCE: In 1965 I started out going to law school and working at the old Merc on Franklin Street part-time. I was a board marker. After I finished law school I had the feeling after watching all these people trading, that I was as smart as they were, if not smarter. . . . I thought I'd just give it a try before I practiced law.

Q: *What was it that first motivated you to start trading? Was it the money or something else?*

BRUCE: I kind of liked the idea of trading in the sense of it being a game. It was a chance to beat people. I remember an old saying that Tony Monterano used to quote. "Money is only a way of keeping score." That always stuck with me.

Q: *Was playing games something you enjoyed when you were a kid? Did you like board games or puzzles?*

BRUCE: No, not really but I used to go to the racetrack. I was never very big on board games, but I used to like horse racing and playing cards.

Q: *In your opinion, what does it take to become a successful trader? What personal characteristics would you say it takes to become a top trader?*

BRUCE: You know, I've looked at all of the people that I know and they come from such diverse backgrounds. You watch somebody like Joel Greenberg and you watch somebody like George Segal, Lloyd Arnold, and Bob Rufenacht. I always thought that the only common thread that ever ran through all of these people was that they all kind of had a gross disregard for money. Look at Bob Rufenacht. I worked for him for several years and watched him go up and down several times. The money never bothered him. It never bothered him to lose it. Everybody says, "If I made a million dollars I'd quit." That mentality will never make a million dollars. I think the real players really and truly don't focus on the money.

Q: *Why do you think that is?*

BRUCE: I just think that people don't trade for the money. They do it because it's a game and a challenge. It goes back to what Tony said. The money is just a way of keeping score. I'm sure it would be different if everyday you had to settle up in cash, but it's just numbers to people. They do it because they love the game.

Q: *Do you think when traders focus on the money it detracts from their ability to trade?*

BRUCE: Well, I personally do. It's tough to trade and say, "I have to make X amount of money." I know because I've been in that position. When I've had obligations. It just seems like when you really try to make money and need it, you never can. When you don't need money, the market gives you money! But, when you need it, boy. The market just has a way of kind of knowing. I'm sure it's got to do with your mental outlook. You start pressing and you're looking for sure things to do and it just doesn't work that way.

Q: *In a sense, what you're saying is—I'm interpreting, so tell me if I'm right, that this gross disregard for money, as you call it, is just not solely focusing on the money. You just really are playing the essence of the game. You're not even looking at the score card. Your just right in there playing present time.*

BRUCE: That's right. It doesn't mean that they're foolhardy, but the money just doesn't enter into it. It's more or less a free spirit kind of a person. We've all seen what Joel did to himself, with the bond market. It surely isn't the money that motivates him.

Of course it sounds silly to say that when you see somebody trading the size that he does. To say, well, he doesn't do it for the money. But, in my heart, I believe he doesn't.

Q: *Bruce, what do you think are some of the psychological barriers to successful trading? I think you've touched on some of them. The idea that people keep pressing too hard and feel they need the money too much. What other factors do you believe are preventing people from being successful?*

BRUCE: I think one of the biggest factors is your psychological make up—you are what you're born as. I was born in Berwyn and for me to go out and buy a $2 million house in Northbrook, I mean that isn't me. I think what happens with many traders is that they kind of get used to a lifestyle. Then, they're forced to keep up the lifestyle. I think you have to be comfortable within yourself and not put yourself against the wall. I think it's important you don't get a bunch of obligations heaped on yourself.

Where you've got to make $20,000 a month to pay a mortgage or some other obligation. It is very important not to burden yourself with psychological pressure. I know this sounds a little simplistic but you have to kind of take the market and just kind of live with it. Be clear about the market and not think about a bunch of other stuff that clouds your focus and causes mental pressure.

Q: *So, the psychological barrier would be that people burden themselves with too many extraneous things and get bogged down with outside concerns that fog their view of the markets?*

BRUCE: Yes. They also get into psychological things and they start to think they're smarter than the market. This is a big mistake.

Q: *Lots of guys measure their degree of smartness according to how much money they make and we all know that's generally not proportionate.*

BRUCE: True. There's a lot of smart people who can't trade a market.

Q: *Do you think a great trader is born that way or do you think someone can be taught to become a great trader?*

BRUCE: That's a good question because I really, in my heart, I think that you're kind of born that way. That's the ability to put the bad news out of your mind and be able to come back. Just from watching people in life, I don't think there's many people that could—I hate to keep going back to Joel, but taking an ass kicking like he did in those bonds and come back after that experience—I don't think it's an acquired trait. I think you're just born with that resilience.

Q: *Bruce, you know what's fascinating? How we learn to talk about these trading experiences to ourselves. For example, Joel doesn't think he was beaten. That's the amazing thing about Joel. Everybody we talked to refers to Joel's "tragedy" and when we asked Joel about it he experienced it completely differently.*

BRUCE: He never felt that! I guess he reasons things out! So, he may have analyzed it out correctly, but something happens and intervenes that changes the analysis and he doesn't feel like he failed. He says to himself I did what I thought was right. Until another external force hits him in the ass.

Along those lines, I don't think you can ever look back at something bad that happened to you and kind of keep re-hashing. You just have to walk away from it and get on to the next trade. I think that's important to people in trading because sometimes people dwell on it. If you want to make it as a trader you have to be able to throw bad experiences over your shoulder and move on. You also have to keep a positive attitude.

Q: *I think that's an interesting insight as well. If you're trading from a perspective of bitterness or anger or revenge in the market, you know you're going to get caught up.*

BRUCE: Or chasing the money that you already lost. It's gone! Forget it. On to the next trade. Watch people. They get a thing in their head and they want to get it back from the same market, the same day, week, or month that they lost it in.

Q: *For you, personally, what was the most challenging psychological barrier that you had to overcome? What kind of internal demons did you have to work through?*

BRUCE: Well, I started out a couple of times and went down. At that time, it was $1,800 and $3,000. I even lost the money my wife had accumulated for a down payment on a house. She was crying! I was just very concerned about what everyone else thought even though I felt I could make it as a trader. I believed my dad was going to be disappointed if I wasn't a lawyer. I had to bring myself around and it was really kind of hard for me at first. Everybody I went to law school with was beginning to practice law but I just felt I had to give trading a chance.

There is another thing I want to mention. When the stock market broke in '87, they caught me with a bunch of cattle. I was soon back to square one. That was the first time I kind of started to feel a little sorry for myself. I said to myself, "all of those years and you pissed it all away on one trade." That's the only time I ever kind of had second thoughts about trading. I put in all this work in here. I said, "You haven't saved a thing." It's not like you're broke. The house is paid but, it just kind of brought the whole thing home about how fast you can get wrecked. It took about three weeks.

Q: *This was '87? After you had been trading for twenty years you felt as though you were starting all over again?*

BRUCE: I wasn't even in the S&Ps. I was in the cattle. I started in '65. So, that's 22 years.

I had to go borrow money. That really is about the only time that I ever felt really down as a trader because I felt I knew I was right, that the cattle market would turn around but I still had to get out of everything. But you know what I did? I just started buying them back in smaller increments and got all the money back when the cattle market came back. But I was pretty down. It was literally like starting from square one. But I knew I was right!

Q: *Is there anything specifically that you said to yourself in order for you to get around to start buying again? I mean, getting out was* *probably a saving grace, but then getting back in is really the reason that you're successful. What is it that you said to yourself or how did you turn yourself around from feeling sorry for yourself to acting decisively?*

BRUCE: I just started like I always had. I bought five loads and then bought ten loads. It was like two weeks later, I had a couple of hundred contracts back on. I think it's kind of like that old thing about after you fall off the horse, you've got to get back on it. I'm a believer that the longer you sit there and feel sorry for yourself, the worse it gets. I just started back trading. Then, I said I'll never, ever in my whole life get over 50 contracts on again. I made that promise! But never kept it. Two weeks later, I had 200 contracts on and I'm aggressively looking to buy more.

Q: *And you were convinced that your opinion of the market was right?*

BRUCE: Absolutely. Once the stock market quit breaking, I said, well, if I'm right, they're going right back up. That was really a traumatic thing for me. It only lasted about two weeks. I was really down on myself, and I usually don't get that way.

Q: *When things are going against you in the market like the cattle trade, what do you visualize, what do you hear, what do you feel?*

BRUCE: I just always think, well, it's only money. I kind of play a game with myself. I say you walked in here broke. You can walk out of here broke, you had a bunch of good years and a hell of a lot of fun!

Q: *If you make a trade in the cattle at 75 cents and as soon as you buy it, the next day it's down 100 points or so, what do you say to yourself?*

BRUCE: I buy more. I don't trade like a lot of people and put them all on at one price. If I was going to trade 100 lots, I'd buy them 10 at a time and sometimes five at a time. I think that's kind of how Joel used to do it. Now you hear a little bigger numbers. A guy like Swinford used to do it that way, too. You know, two, two, two. I always thought that that was a good approach to it and not get the whole mother load on at one price.

Q: *You're basically a fundamentalist. So, you're looking at what you expect the market to do.*

BRUCE: But, not like in Joel's sense. I don't sit down and crunch the numbers like he does. I'll talk to people. I have certain people that I respect. I kind of work a little bit on the technical stuff.

Q: *At what point do you say you've had enough?*

BRUCE: I don't know. I just all of a sudden say we're done fighting this deal and kick them out. I'm pretty stubborn in the market. Bellies go against me $5 and I don't trade a lot of bellies, maybe 25 loads. It doesn't bother me.

Q: *Does it bother you to be wrong?*

BRUCE: Yeah. It bothers me to be wrong in my analysis. It doesn't bother me when the market moves against me. It just bothers me when the eventual outcome is not what I thought it should be.

Q: *You're not bothered so much by the fact that the market goes a day or two against you as long as you feel the market's still the way you're expecting it to act. Are you watching the individual ticks in the market?*

BRUCE: I watch them, but it kind of doesn't register to me. I kind of mind trade the thing. I'll say, well, the bellies went to

$45 this morning, so they should come back down around the half and then hold. Then, if they are any good, pull back above $45. But I never do anything about it. I kind of take a little bit of pleasure just being right in my analysis of what I think it should do.

Q: *When things are really going well for you in the market, when you feel like you're untouchable, what are you saying to yourself?*

BRUCE: I think it's always the same thing. You always want to buy more. I found out that one of my faults is that if I leave the money in there, I always do buy more. I think you have to get the money out of there for awhile or else you think you're impervious, you know.

Q: *Do you ever feel like you get caught up in the euphoria of a trade?*

BRUCE: I don't know. I really and truly thought the April cattle were going to $85, and I thought they were going to close above that and they didn't. But, they got close, and when they broke, that made me mad. I guess I do get caught up in the euphoria. It was so close. I think they got to, like, $84.30. Everybody told me I was nuts, they said they'd never take the cattle to $85, and I just kind of wish they would have gotten there, so I could have told them I told you so.

Q: *Do you feel down when the market's going against you? Do you get depressed?*

BRUCE: No!

Q: *How do you keep your state of mind up?*

BRUCE: I always kind of say to myself in the morning, kind of convince myself, that I'm going to have a good day. And even if it isn't good, I always kind of look on the bright side of everything. I'm really the eternal optimist. Which I think is essential,

I mean that's like the essential ingredient in being a good trader; you just have to be positive.

Q: *What are some of the beliefs that you have about yourself as a trader? Don't be afraid to be immodest. We're really trying to look at what people's true beliefs are about themselves.*

BRUCE: I know I've got an ability, not to be influenced by other people. I can sit there, like in this company (Packers), I would be long and everybody will get on the other side, short. That doesn't bother me. I know I've got confidence in what I think. I also have, I think, an uncanny ability to read people.

I can kind of read the market. Like, when it looks the worst, it doesn't really bother me. And I think to myself, boy, this is the place where I would be the scardest. That's about the only thing that I can think of. I certainly do have the ability to pull the trigger. I don't sit there and think about it and I don't price them 25 points lower. If I decide to buy them, I just buy the first bunch to get started. That to me is important. To get the first bunch and then I start to look for areas to add to them.

Q: *If you bought that first bunch and say you were right, that's great! But let's say you buy that first bunch and the market is immediately 100 points against you, then what . . . ?*

BRUCE: I say I'd look at that as a plus, then.

Q: *So, you can buy more?*

BRUCE: Because like I say, if I was a 100 car trader, I wouldn't buy the full 100 when I thought it was time to buy; I'd do ten cars just to get started.

Q: *Is there anyone that you think of who has served as a role model for you as a trader?*

BRUCE: Bob Rufenacht (the "R" in RB&H, Inc.) always impressed me. I kind of saw in Rufenacht that devil-may-care attitude. Rufenacht taught me not to be scared of the numbers you put on. I also watched Glen Bromagen (the "B" in RB&H, Inc.) who is a pretty good student of the market. But it isn't a game to him. He wants to make money. I kind of took a little bit of Bromagen and a little bit of Rufenacht. I always admired Bromagen's discipline, and I admired Rufenacht's attitude.

Q: *What words of advice or encouragement can you offer to a new trader, to someone who really wants to become successful as a futures trader? What would you tell him?*

BRUCE: I know one thing. You can't trade with the rent money and put yourself under the pressure of having to make money. I know that it's changed a tremendous amount with this fund business. It used to be when you could call a hog market a dollar higher when everybody else thought it was going to be lower. It doesn't happen that way anymore! You should always keep a positive attitude. You cannot have psychological pressure on yourself. If you do, you better be able to put it out of your mind. I think there's very few people that can do that. That's why there are so few really great traders.

PART IV

THE PSYCHOLOGY OF TECHNICAL ANALYSIS

A Random Walk Down
a Crowded Lane

One of our fundamental assumptions is that futures markets are not random. For our purposes, we define random as having no directional bias over time. Any trader who has ever studied simple charts can easily verify the upward or downward bias of most markets. This bias within a defined time frame is referred to as a trend. Trends can be seen as market psychology at work.

The classic definition of a trend: "higher highs and higher lows," has a strong psychological foundation. Emotionally and intellectually, there is great comfort for the trading public when a market makes new highs, falls off, and fails to make new lows in a particular period of time. Traders then become willing buyers at higher price levels and sellers are only attracted to the market at even higher levels. Of course, the opposite is true for downward trending markets.

Whether the markets are trending up or down, or for that matter, not at all, there is an opportunity for profit. The top traders have all devised some methodology or combination of methods and techniques to trade markets with consistency. It doesn't matter if the trader is a fundamentalist or a technician, each one has developed a unique "solution" to markets. This "solution" we call a trading system. It's important to understand that trading systems are nothing more than an attempt to put order into a chaotic world. The world of futures.

The trading system gives the trader the ability to control his or her emotional and mental states rather than allowing them to control him or her. A system is a disciplined method for organizing dynamic, ever-changing market phenomena.

A successful trading system is composed of a number of independent elements that are joined together to make the whole. These elements are discrete, however mutually interactive. They are:

- Trend Identification
- Entry and/or Exit
- Money Management

Before we move on to a detailed discussion of trading systems and classical chart analysis, we must caution the reader that our focus is not on an in-depth study of the technical aspects of trading markets, but rather it is on how our emotional states and the psychological skills we have learned relate to using the trading system. As we have clearly seen, it is the innergame of the trader that determines if the system or the specific analytical methods of choice will be successful.

Chapter Fifteen

Trends and the Efficient Market Theory

It would seem that if markets were really the efficient mechanisms that some academics propose, the markets would find their proper levels in one full leap. This obviously is not the case.

Trend Identifiers

The primary methods of trend identification are:

- Linear—trendlines
- Moving averages
- Channel breakouts

Simple trend lines are usually drawn from low to low to establish an uptrend, or from high to high to establish a downtrend. (See Figure 15-1.) Variations on this theme are possible by using closes instead of lows or averaging daily ranges and using those points as references.

The oldest and best known method of establishing a trend is the moving average. (See Figure 15-2.) In its simplest form, a moving average is usually obtained by adding up a series of closes and dividing the sum by the number of days used in the series. The result is a smoothing of the series of numbers and an

Figure 15-1

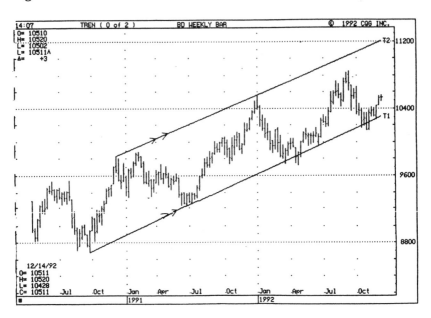

© Copyright 1993 CQG INC.

effective method of trend identification. Many variations are possible, such as varying the number of days in the series, using an average of the daily range, using highs and lows and even changing the value of the most recent days compared to the oldest days. The most obvious use of the moving average is in identifying that a trend is established when the close (or whatever variable you choose) is over the average (or under), thereby signalling direction.

The channel breakout method can be used on its own or in conjunction with the other methods. (See Figure 15-3.) We define a channel as a series of days or weeks that is contained

Figure 15-2

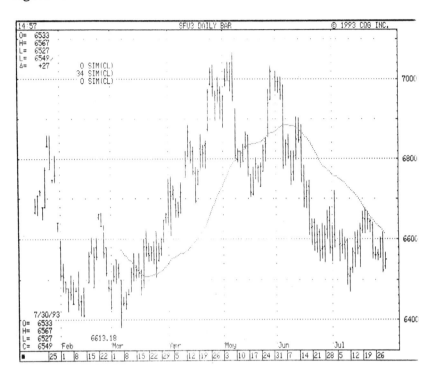

© Copyright 1993 CQG INC.

within an area of highs and lows (or average of highs and lows). When a market moves through an area which has been established over a period of time it then signals a trend.

The point to remember is that the individual trader's inclination and personal psychology limits the potential use of the above concepts of trend identification. Of course, the opposite is also true.

Figure 15-3

© Copyright 1993 CQG INC.

Entry and/or Exit

- Fast moving averages
- Highs and lows
- Retracement

Once a trend has been identified, the trader must decide how best to enter the market. One commonly used device is the fast moving average. (See Figure 15-4.) A fast moving average is an average that is composed of a relatively short number of days or weeks. Because it responds quickly to market movement we have labeled it "fast." A simple use of this average is to enter the market if the price is above the fast average and has already established an uptrend. An option is to buy the market as it comes to the fast average and exit the market when it violates this point.

Figure 15-4

© Copyright 1993 CQG INC.

The use of highs and lows is common among traders. When a trend is established, new highs or new lows can signal resumption of market movement in the direction of the trend. (See Figure 15-5.)

Some traders prefer to wait for the market to retrace its move to either the area of the trend change or to the moving average, or the trendline. There are many variations available to

Figure 15-5

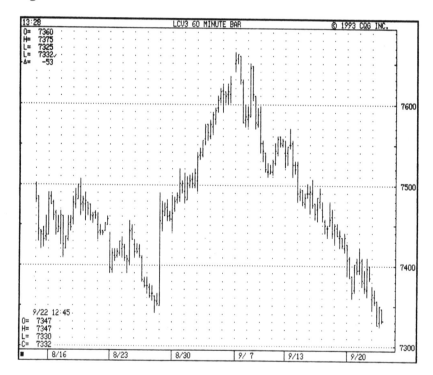

© Copyright 1993 CQG INC.

allow a trader to incorporate the concept of retracement into a system. (See Figure 15-6.)

Figure 15-6

© Copyright 1993 CQG INC.

Chapter Sixteen

Money Management

Proper money management technique is the most difficult element of a successful system. And yet, because of the enormous leverage used in futures, it is without doubt the most vital. It is possible that a system built without money management in it, even one that is ninety percent accurate, can wipe out your equity. The most common emotional and psychological barriers which prevent trading success stem from poor money management. All the top traders we have interviewed have come to terms with the concept of equity management and have developed a consistent methodology to deal with it.

The opportunity for the extraordinary success that is possible in futures trading derives from the leverage. But it's also the leverage that makes success so difficult. Too few traders acknowledge this and fewer still incorporate any methodology to protect themselves from disaster.

Many of the axioms we have listed earlier deal with the concept of money management. For example;

- Take small losses, let your profits run.
- Don't let a profit turn into a loss.
- Don't risk all your equity on a single trade.

The following table illustrates the rationale for many of these axioms.

The Mathematics of Money Management

Equity	Losses at 500	Net loss	Profit at 1500	Net Profit	Net Result
10,000	6	3000	4	6000	3000
10,000	7	3500	3	4500	1000
10,000	8	4000	2	3000	(1000)

We can see in the above table how a system designed to take small losses and large profits will give us a positive result even if we are correct only three out of ten trades. If the system runs into a series of eight out of ten losses, our equity drawdown is still relatively small, ten percent of trading equity.

Understanding the key elements that are necessary to build a trading system gives us the framework in which we can exploit market opportunities. It allows us to utilize the psychological skills we have learned and complements the individual requirements of our own personalities.

We are reminded of the story of the trader who sat in a boardroom with several other traders and boasted of a most unusual system. This trader would carry an empty Coke bottle around and every so often put it to his ear and claim that he received buy and sell instructions from aliens in a spaceship from outer space. When the trades turned out correct he basked in the glow of success telling everyone who would listen about his good fortune and alien friends. However, when the trades were unsuccessful he would quickly get out of the position and claim that sun spot interference caused distortions which made him misunderstand the instructions from his alien friends.

The elements of this successful system were devilishly simple. He made a trade, took large profits and small losses. It's certainly one way to trade, though not one we recommend.

Chapter Seventeen

Classical Chart Analysis

The simple uptrend line (Figure 17-1) graphically illustrates the "higher highs, higher lows" definition of an uptrend. The trendline is drawn from a low to the next low and carried forward to await the price movement over time. After the fact, the trendline appears to be remarkably successful for so simple a concept.

Whether the trendline itself becomes a self-fulfilling prophecy or it really is a linear representation of the trend is not important. How we can profit from this repeated market action is our focus. And it can consistently be successful except for one thing—the psychological barriers that prevent most of us from using this device with consistency and discipline. Let's examine what is happening and how we might create a method to use the trendline.

After we have drawn a trendline, the opportunity to use it comes as the market is falling into it and allows the trader to buy a breaking market. Psychologically, buying the market at this stage requires (1) belief in the area of the line, (2) confidence to buy when everyone is selling, and (3) accepting the possibility that you may be wrong and will be forced to take a loss.

What is required here is refocusing how we see this opportunity. If we were to develop a simple trading system using all the elements stated above, we could determine our trend with points 1 and 2 and place a buy at point 3. The first psychological barrier to overcome is to commit to buying at or near the trend-

---

Figure 17-1

© Copyright 1993 CQG INC.

line. The next psychological barrier to overcome is to decide when to exit the market. This is the most difficult to deal with. We must shift our focus from "they are going to get me out" to "it's better to take a small loss knowing this trade has defined risk and unlimited upside potential."

A number of things happen when we employ this strategy. The first is we preserve our equity. The second is we have no position and should be able to make a more objective decision about the market in the future. By conditioning ourselves to utilize this discipline on a consistent basis, we allow for opportunities where profits will run later.

Another element that we can introduce into our system is reentry. We have found that one of the reasons traders hesitate to get out of a market is that they harbor a fear that they will be taken out of the market and they will never be able to reenter.

The reentry puts you back into the market. If, for example, our reentry is based on the trendline, we will reestablish our position as soon and as often as the market satisfies our criteria. These simple elements of a trading system will be refined, adjusted, and fine-tuned over time. But, whatever approach we employ—we must be consistent!

We know there are those traders who will focus on the market breaking the trendline, signalling a change of direction. Great! However, bear in mind the approach is the same. The trendline gives us a lot of information and we must respect the market's ability or inability to hold it. One of our favorite situations is a close under an established trendline that is immediately followed by a close above that very line. This is a high percentage, defined risk, buy signal. Here is a market that has violated it's uptrend line, chasing weak longs and attracting short sellers The market's inability to follow through, reverse and resume it's course shaking out weak shorts and attracting new longs signals a very clear buying opportunity.

The analytical possibilities that exist when employing a trendline in moving markets are limited only by the trader's imagination. The same holds true with moving averages. A moving average is basically a non-linear representation of a trendline. The moving average gives the trader the ability to define what constitutes a trend and allows him or her to further personalize a trading system. By changing the number of closes in the series the trader will change how quickly the average responds to changes in the market. As the market moves over the average and continues away from it, a trend is in place. How the trader uses the elements of a system to operate effectively in that trend is based on personal levels of conviction, confidence, and the trader's own state of mind.

The most difficult market to trade is the one with no trend at all; however, a market that is not trending, with no upward or downward bias may be said to be in a sideways trend. This trend creates additional opportunities and profitable strategies can be devised. As we will see later in a discussion about support and resistance, market psychology plays an important role in creating this sideways trend or channel. (See Figure 17-2.)

As a market moves to a level that attracts buyers, it will soon stabilize and trade away from a price near where sellers become more reluctant to sell. The rally peaks when sellers are attracted by the higher prices and weak or short-term longs begin to exit. The market then retreats to the previous lows where the process repeats itself. This market action can be repeated for days, weeks, months, and years. One opportunity resides in first determining that the market is in a channel and then creating a system to profit from it.

Another approach is to wait for the upper or lower boundaries of the channel to be penetrated thus signalling a significant change in direction. The ability of the market to move out of the channel indicates a change in market psychology. In an upside breakout, sellers now find themselves overwhelmed by aggressive buyers who are willing to pay higher prices. The opposite, of course is true for a downside breakout. When either of these events occur the trader's trend-following rules are the keys that open the lock of market opportunity.

Figure 17-2

© Copyright 1993 CQG INC.

Support and Resistance— Fear, Greed, and Hope

It's fear, greed, and hope that create this market pattern.

The channel pattern described above is a good example of support and resistance. It's easy to see the dynamics of the market as it repeatedly holds the lows and highs over an extended period of time.

Now let's examine what is taking place as the market breaks out of the channel, in this instance on the upside. Aggressive buying and shortcovering drives the market to a point that attracts new sellers and profit taking longs. This begins the market's normal retracement. However, as the market sets back towards the area of the top of the channel, we can examine the forces at play. Former buyers or potential buyers who saw the market move through the channel highs and missed the opportunity begin to buy again near those highs. At the same time, short sellers who did not exit quickly enough now see the opportunity to buy back their positions close to their entry point. This combined buying at the channel high area establishes support. Similarly a breakdown below the channel lows and subsequent rally forms resistance. Each of these occurrences is an opportunity to enter the market in the direction of the trend with reduced risk.

A variation on this idea of channel support and resistance is the trendline support or resistance. After a trendline has been broken (see Figure 17-3), a retracement back to the trendline forms support or resistance. One of the more reliable patterns we have seen is called the "fan." (See Figure 17-4.) This pattern is usually three trendlines and retracements which precedes a substantial move. The same market psychology recurs at higher and higher levels where the market doesn't retrace at all.

Retracements

One of the more difficult aspects of trading for many traders is to develop the confidence to buy a breaking market or to sell a market rally. Of course, in our discussion we're assuming a trend has been established. We have seen above that support and resistance areas offer some benchmarks or reference points.

Figure 17-3

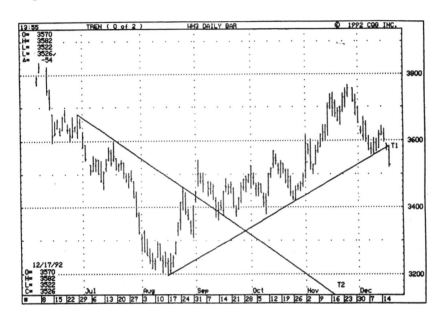

© Copyright 1993 CQG INC.

There is however, another trading method to take advantage of the market's normal retracements. Markets tend to retrace a third, a half, or two thirds of the previous move. (See Figure 17-5.) Many traders get caught up in exact numbers (e.g., .382, .684, etc.) and forget that a few ticks is not meaningful in a dynamic and fluid marketplace. If a market retraces fifty percent of a previous move and shows signs of finding support then the trader has a lot of information with which to make a high percentage, low risk trade.

We have now demonstrated a few tangible ways with which to follow the famous axiom "buy low, sell high." You can look for retracement breaks or rallies that are near support or resis-

Figure 17-4

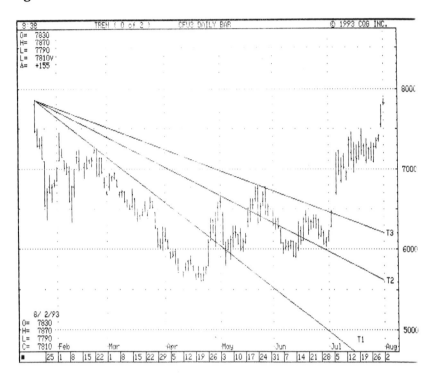

© Copyright 1993 CQG INC.

tance, and are a significant percentage of the previous move in order to enter the market.

May the axioms be with you!

More about Trends

A discussion about trends is important because all the top traders we have spoken to seem to know or believe they know

Figure 17-5

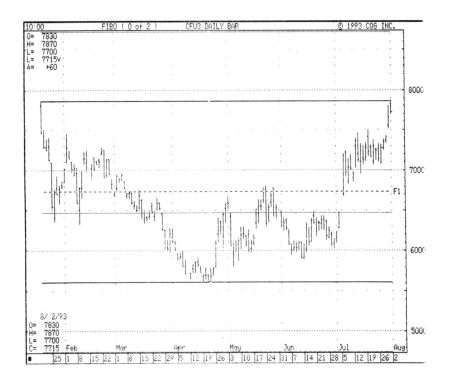

© Copyright 1993 CQG INC.

where the markets are relative to the trend. For example, the market is bottoming, topping, retracing, etc.

Each major up or down trend has three phases. They are:

- Accumulation
- Main Phase
- Distribution

The accumulation phase of a market is characterized by low prices, light volume, small open interest, and small daily ranges. On occasion, the market might have a flurry of activity but quickly reverts to the doldrums. This is a period when everything about the market seems negative or uninteresting. Downside becomes limited as buyers begin to establish positions and sellers await better prices. As the market rallies away from the bottom, some weak longs and expectant sellers put a lid on the market which gives the buyers more opportunity. This continues until the market enters the next phase.

The main phase begins with a breakout and a sustained rally above the bottom area. (See Figure 17-6.) No apparent fundamental change or increased public awareness has caused this rally and trading has expanded but is not volatile. During this phase the reasons for the trend become more public and trading interest increases. Volatility and daily ranges expand and the public at large is now convinced of higher prices. This leads to the third phase.

Long-term buyers who accumulated this market near the lows use the public excitement to liquidate their long positions. This is the distribution phase. As Jeffrey Silverman put it, "Feed the ducks when they're quacking." This phase is marked by large swings in the market, record open interest, high volume, and media interest. It's the beginning of the major downtrend.

Reversal Patterns—Santayana Was Right

Traders who don't learn from history will continue to buy tops and sell bottoms.

The chart patterns that are created by trader psychology during accumulation and distribution are called reversal patterns. (See Figure 17-7.) These patterns are seen time and time

Figure 17-6

© Copyright 1993 CQG INC.

again. Rounded bottoms and tops, V or spike bottoms and tops, double or triple bottoms or tops, and head and shoulders bottoms and tops are the most common reversal chart patterns. Bottoms usually are quieter and take a longer time to develop but on occasion a spike or double bottom occurs in a short period of time as the market extends beyond an expected low.

Tops, on the other hand, are more often than not volatile, quick to form, and accompanied by lots of noise and attention. (See Figure 17-7.)

Figure 17-7

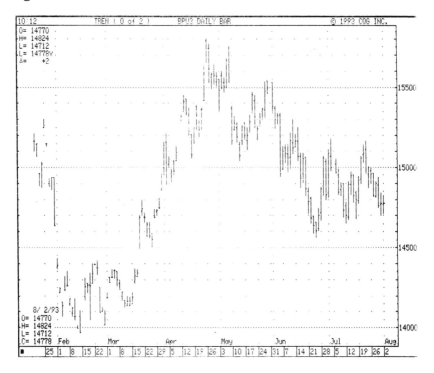

One interesting chart pattern is that of the reversal day. Sometimes called a "key reversal," it is a high or contract high followed by a lower close for the day or week. This market action usually typifies weak buying by longs and short covering by sellers who cover on the new highs. When this buying is exhausted, the market is vulnerable and falls. This action may or may not signal a top but is a high percentage pattern for a continuation of the break.

Continuation Patterns—Midlife Crises

This pattern is like midlife. It can be stressful and confusing. Continuation patterns generally present themselves halfway through the trend.

During the main phase of a trending market certain patterns develop repeatedly. We call these continuation patterns because they usually are mere pauses in the established trend. Their names are indicative of their shapes: triangles, flags and rectangles. (See Figure 17-8.)

After a market moves significantly in one direction it tends to pause as new sellers attracted by the runup and short-term longs responding to their profits begin to sell. This sell off finds support and begins its climb to the high of this move, but falls short as more sellers take advantage of the rally. This next break finds buyers at a higher level than the last sell off did and another rally begins only to be met by sellers at a lower level than the last rally high. This tug-of-war over a few days or weeks begins to form one of three basic triangles: the symmetrical triangle, named because of the similar ascending and descending lows and highs; the ascending triangle because of the higher lows and equal highs; and the descending triangle because of the lower highs and equal lows. Traders can use this pattern in various ways. Buying the reaction to the low end of the triangle offers an opportunity to enter with the trend or as some traders like to do, buy on the break out over the trendline drawn from one triangle high to the next triangle high or a new high for this move.

Flags are similar patterns except that they are formed by lower highs and lower lows. Many traders make the mistake of buying a market during this pattern and using a new low as a stop area. If you are confident that you are in a continuation pattern, you must assume that this could be a flag and expect a

Figure 17-8

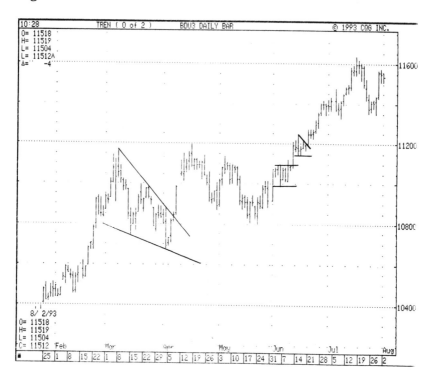

© Copyright 1993 CQG INC.

new low. It's the weak longs and over-anxious short sellers who set this pattern up. (See Figure 17-8.)

Rectangles are channels created by equal highs and lows and as the market is again tugged at in turn by buyers and sellers in a fixed range. (See Figure 17-8.)

The point to remember is one's psychological skills of enhanced belief and confidence are what enable personal involvement in the market at these times.

Gaps

Gaps, that is, price action that produces a higher low than the previous high or a lower high than the previous low (see Figure 17-9) are an important indicator of market strength or weakness. There are several types of gaps: the common gap, the breakaway gap, the runaway gap, and the exhaustion gap. The common gap appears inside a larger formation such as a channel or triangle and does not have much significance. The breakaway gap gets its name because it usually occurs when a market is moving through important support or resistance areas or trendlines. (See Figure 17-9.) If a market closes near a resistance area but not above it and the next day opens sharply higher it creates a gap. The market now has an area where no trading has taken place, and poses additional questions to traders. Those traders who sold against the previous highs must now decide whether to cover at much higher levels (that is, much higher than they had anticipated) or to wait for a market retreat back to the area of previous highs. On the other hand, potential longs must decide whether to wait for the retracement or to join the already aggressive buying that is taking place. This scenario sets up the age-old question about the importance of "filling in" the gap area. To our way of thinking, this is merely our old market retracement to a former support area. If the market is very strong then the gap may be partially filled or not filled at all. Some traders focus on the idea that a filled-in gap shows market weakness. We believe that analysis of subsequent action is essential to determine if the market is still in the uptrend.

A runaway gap occurs most often from a continuation pattern and is sometimes called a "measuring gap" because the subsequent move's objective is about the size of the previous move to the continuation pattern. (See Figure 17-9.)

Figure 17-9

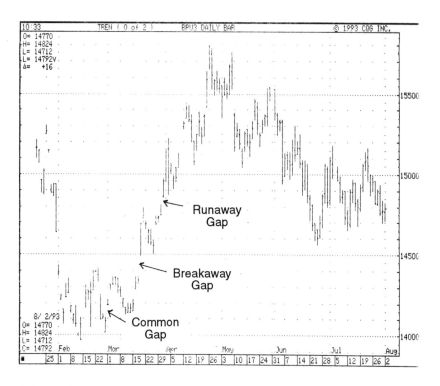

© Copyright 1993 CQG INC.

The exhaustion gap occurs after sharp and volatile moves and sometimes in a series of two or three. (See Figure 17-10.) A most interesting result of an exhaustion gap is the "island reversal." (See Figure 17-10.) This is formed by an exhaustion gap followed by a another gap in the opposite direction, leaving the top day or week looking like an island. This pattern has a high reliability and quite often signals long-term tops and bottoms.

These gap patterns as well as the various technical formations we have discussed comprise the language with which the

Figure 17-10

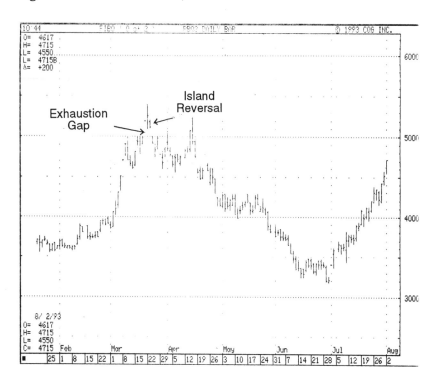

© Copyright 1993 CQG INC.

market gives the trader information. But what is most important is this: it is necessary for the trader to effectively communicate this information to himself, and to be psychologically able to utilize this information to produce winning results.

We know there are many books that concentrate on technical analysis for developing systems and utilizing specific technical strategies and techniques. What we believe we offer in *The Innergame of Trading* is how to overcome the psychological barriers that routinely confront the trader at the moment of decision at critical junctures in the market.

Furthermore, by applying the psychological skills that we have presented here, the trader can easily overcome inhibiting psychological pressures by maintaining defined objectives, clarity of focus, and a consistently resourceful state of mind.

Successful trading has more to do with knowing how to adapt your psychological makeup to a specific market strategy than possessing any particular trading system. This is our belief based on forty years' combined experience as traders and confirmed by our interviews with the top traders in the futures industry.

PART V

WINNING VERSUS LOSING

Chapter Eighteen

Principles of Successful Trading

- Define your loss
- Take profits and losses at your objectives
- Believe in yourself and in unlimited market possibilities
- Have a well-defined money management system
- Don't buy price
- Don't take tips
- Don't trade angry or euphoric
- Trade aggressively at your numbers and points
- Be prepared for breakouts
- Focus on opportunities
- Consistently apply your trading strategies and rules
- Be highly motivated and goal oriented
- Always trade in a state of self-trust and confidence

The motto of the Nike Corporation is "There is no finish line," and so it is with trading. We have discussed in great detail the factors which separate winning from losing. We have seen how the top performing traders represent trading experiences to themselves in order to achieve excellent results. In addition, we have seen how committed traders who have strong enough desires and are willing to "pay the price" can be successful at trading by understanding their motives, setting goals, developing winning trading beliefs, and strategies and by conditioning themselves to consistently utilize the psychological skills learned in *The Innergame of Trading*. Moreover, in the chapter on technical analysis, we described how these psychological skills can be routinely applied within the framework of conventional technical market analysis. As a participant in one of our seminars once said "Success is that old ABC—ability, breaks, and courage." We feel this well sums up the game of trading.

All of the traders we interviewed initially experienced great difficulty and frustration, but what sets them apart is that they never allowed themselves to experience failure. That is to say, they refused to represent their trading experience, no matter how negative, as personal failure. Leo Melamed reported that he was broke three times before he became successful. As Orison Swett Marden observed, "Failure! There is no such word in all the bright lexicon of speech, unless you yourself have written it there! There is no such thing as failure except to those who accept and believe in failure."

We would like to share someone's life history with you:

At the age of 21 he failed in business.

At the age of 22 he lost a state legislative race.

At the age of 24 he failed again in business.

At the age of 26 his lover died.

At the age of 27 he had a nervous breakdown.

At the age of 34 he lost a congressional race.

At the age of 36 he lost another congressional race.

At the age of 45 he lost a senatorial race.

At the age of 49 he again lost a senatorial race.

But at the age of 52 he was elected President of the United States.

This was Abraham Lincoln.

The point is, experience is how we choose to represent an event to ourselves, whether we are running for the presidency or committing ourselves to becoming a consistently winning trader.

In earlier sections we have discussed the importance of accepting losses as a key factor in successful trading. We have also heard from the top traders who repeatedly underscore this point. As George Segal put it, "If you can't accept a loss and are afraid to make a trade then trading is just not for you. It doesn't mean you're a bad person; it just means you should consider doing something else." In addition, we have seen the importance of accepting profits. As Joseph Siegel explained, "You must allow yourself to maximize your positions and when the markets reach your objective, overcome your 'fear' to get out."

In addition to accepting losses and profits, there is one more thing that you need to accept if you choose to be a winning trader—*you*. You must learn what market factors trigger your self-limiting states so that you can alter your beliefs and behaviors by using the psychological skills that we have learned. This will enable you to move easily from inhibiting to resourceful states of mind.

Chapter Nineteen

Characteristics of Winning

The following list indicates the psychological characteristics of winning states that require ongoing conditioning.

Psychological Characteristics of Winning States

- Expect the best of yourself
- Establish a personal standard of excellence
- Create an internal atmosphere for success
- Communicate effectively with yourself
- Know yourself

Expect the Best of Yourself

In our experience, most traders, in a psychological sense, don't trade to win. They trade not to lose! When you trade not to lose you can never achieve peak performance. In order to derive the best of yourself, you must take risk (defined); you must take decisive and automatic action and do everything in your power to win. Expecting the best of yourself at all times will allow you to create and maintain a resourceful psychological state regardless of trading circumstances or conditions. The real test of course is not when things are going great for you but rather, when things get tough, the pressure is high, and the trading seems to be spinning out of control. It is at these times it is essential to expect the best of yourself based on your commitment, hard work, and discipline. In other words, confidence based on competence will allow you to stay relaxed, focused, concentrated, highly motivated, and most importantly, in control.

Having said that, we're reminded of a story we once heard about Arthur Rubinstein, the famous pianist. When Rubinstein was in his nineties he was asked if his hands ever hurt when he played. Rubinstein thought for a moment and then answered, "Only when I hit the wrong notes!" When times are difficult, that is the true test of how successful you are in applying the psychological skills of the innergame of trading. The literature is rife with a wealth of psychological studies that report the importance of positive perception on performance. How you perceive yourself will ultimately determine your outcome. Trading constantly presents us with obstacles and opportunities. Expecting the best of yourself is the best means for dealing constructively with both of them.

Establish a Personal Standard of Excellence

Knute Rockne used to say, "Show me a good loser and I'll show you a loser." Successful trading is all about winning, internal and external. The key to successful trading, as we have seen, is to feel like a winner even though you may be temporarily losing, representing the loss as part of an overall process of confidence and competence.

Establishing a personal standard of excellence is a minimum standard. The top traders have all learned this. They constantly read and study and refine their techniques. They do what is necessary to consistently win. As one top trader put it, "I try to improve my trading by 1 percent every day. At the end of the year this is a staggering number."

Understanding your motives and establishing concrete goals will allow you to maintain a consistently high standard of performance. By defining exactly what steps are necessary to secure your goals, you can routinely adopt appropriate actions. As Thomas Huxley observed, "The great end of life is not knowledge but action." Adopting a standard of excellence will permit you to achieve your trading goals and experience the success you are capable of attaining. It was Grant Tinker who said, "First we will be best, and then we will be first." This philosophy applies as much to trading as it does to getting top television ratings. Hard work and discipline and belief all combine to establish the standard that will guarantee ultimate success.

"The reason a lot of people do not recognize opportunity is because it usually goes around wearing overalls looking like hard work."

— Thomas A. Edison

Create an Internal Environment for Success

In order to be successful as a trader you must create an atmosphere that is pleasant and comfortable where your trading can flourish. You must also create a positive psychological dialogue with yourself based on empowering imagery of a visual, auditory, and kinesthetic nature. This will result in a high level of self-confidence and focused concentration. Trading will also be experienced as effortless, highly enjoyable, and in control.

Formula for Creating a Successful Internal Dialogue

- Create imagery that respects you. That makes you feel important.
- Don't criticize, condemn, or complain. Bitching and moaning won't help.
- Keep your ego out of trading. Concentrate on how you can develop as a trader. How you can increase your base of knowledge and improve your execution strategies
- Work to constantly improve. Work for excellence not perfection. Excellence provides results, perfection produces ulcers.
- Concentrate on solutions. Don't reiterate problems.
- Identify your own strengths and weaknesses. Learn from your mistakes.
- Take personal responsibility for all decisions . . . not just the good trades.
- Develop a system for referring back to and analyzing trades you have made.
- Invest your time wisely. Concentrate on what works. It is essential that you direct your focus on the practical and not solely on the theoretical.

- And most importantly, always remember there is a to-morrow. Don't try to do it all today!

Communicate Effectively with Yourself

When we conduct trading seminars we always offer the mnemonic TORCH FIRE to represent the essential ingredients in communicating effectively with yourself.

- Trust—Learn to trust yourself. Follow your instincts, you will be pleasantly surprised.
- Open—Be open-minded.
- Respect—Respect yourself by not speaking harshly to yourself. Stay positive.
- Challenge—Set goals and challenges for yourself that are realistic and will help to build confidence.
- Humor—Have a sense of humor. Remember trading is a game; it can be a lot of fun.
- Faith—Have ultimate faith (belief) in yourself and your proven methodology.
- Interested—Keep your interest level high by constantly improving.
- Results—Be results oriented.
- Enthusiasm—Be in the right state of mind. Enthusiastic and energized. Enjoy yourself.

Communicating effectively with yourself will bring out your ability and allow you to succeed by making the right trading decisions.

"Your mind is a sacred enclosure into which nothing harmful can enter except by your permission."

—Ralph Waldo Emerson

Know Yourself

"The easiest thing to be in the world is you. The most difficult thing to be is what other people want you to be."

— Anonymous

There is an ancient Talmudic expression which states "To change and to improve are two vastly different things." In order to improve at trading or anything else, you must begin by knowing yourself, learning what are the things that motivate your actions. What role do fear, doubt, and worry play in your life? How important is it for you to be successful? The more you understand about yourself the more effective you will be at trading and everything else. Zig Ziglar used to say in his seminars, "You are what you are and where you are because of what has gone into your mind; you change what you are and where you are by changing what goes into your mind" By learning what your current trading motives are, you can establish goals and a system of belief that will assure success.

We have seen what sets the top traders apart. We have learned from them, in their own words, what is their syntax for successful trading. We have also discussed how to apply the innergame of trading when utilizing technical analysis.

By directing our focus and by conditioning ourselves to have an ongoing positive internal dialogue in terms of our specific beliefs, feelings, and imagery, we can choose how we as individuals internally represent external market phenomena. We can shape our goals and strategies to bring us closer to the trading success that is within our grasp.

"Go as far as you can see, and when you get there, you will see further."

— Anonymous

On the south side of Chicago a young girl looked out her bedroom window and was mesmerized by the vast openness and possibilities of space. She was fascinated by what she saw and felt deep within herself that someday she would travel in space. And no matter that all the astronauts were male and white and she was female and black, she just believed in the future she too would explore space. There were many detours, real and imagined, but despite them all she just refused to be deterred from her strong commitment and belief in her ultimate goal. On September 17, 1992, Mae C. Jemison took off into space as a member of shuttle *Endeavor's* crew. The hard work and discipline had made her dream come true.

Success comes to those who dream, and to those who make their dreams come true—and the sky is no longer the limit.

Trading can take you as far and as high as you want to go. It requires commitment, hard work, discipline, and exacting focus and state of mind. The winning edge is inside all of us. It is there to be tapped like an undeveloped oil well. The top traders have learned how to cultivate this natural resource. They have learned how to win at the game of trading and at the same time maintain high levels of self-esteem and achieve enduring personal fulfillment.

As we have stated before, the skills learned in *The Innergame of Trading* apply far beyond the arena of trading. There is application for these skills in every aspect of personal endeavor and human activity. As the English essayist Sydney Smith observed: "A great deal of talent is lost in the world for want of a little courage. Every day sends to their graves obscure men whom timidity prevented from making a first effort; who, if they could have been induced to begin, would in all probability have gone to great lengths in the career of fame. The fact is that to do anything in the world worth doing, we must not stand back shivering and thinking of the cold and danger, but jump in and scramble through as well as we can."

Onward to successful trading!

Index

A

Accumulation, 179, 180
Achievement, 57
  see Goal, Personal
Action(s), 19, 24-25, 72, 197
  see Market, Price
  plan, development, 13, 14
Agatstein, Gene, 12, 71, 74, 78, 85
Analysis, 61, 152, 153
  see Chart, Classical, Fundamental,
    Technical
Anxiety control, 8
Approach, inconsistency, 70
Arnold, Lloyd, 146
Attention, focus, 111
Attitude, 119, 121, 123, 155
  see Negative, Positive
Audio imagery, 63
Auditory, 71, 198
Avenue of excellence, 46
Average, 163
  see Moving
Averaging, 115, 161
Axioms, 169, 177–78
  see Market, Trading

B

Backs, 101
Barriers, see Emotional, Psychological
Baruch, Bernard, 72, 128, 132, 133,
  141
Behavior
  see Market, Modeling, Trading

patterns, constructing, 15, 16
Behavioral
  conditioning, 112
  psychology, 112
Belief
  see Limiting, Market, Personal,
    Positive, Positive/empower-
    ing, Self-limiting, Universal
  lock, 9, 10
  power, 19-20
  system, 70
  see Winners/losers
Bias, 174
Boston-Strangled, 9, 10
Bottom(s), 180–82
Breaking market, 171
Breakout
  see Channel, Downside
  catching, 9, 11, 16, 25
  preparation, 193
Bromagen, Glen, 155
Buffet, Warren, 141
Buying opportunity, 173

C

Capital
  see Trading
  preservation, 7, 12
Channel, 174, 176
  breakouts, 161, 162
  pattern, 175
Chart
  analysis, see Classical
  pattern, 182

reading, 102
Chicago Mercantile Exchange (CME, Merc), 69, 87, 89, 107, 108, 120
Classical chart analysis, 160, 171–188
Commitment, 15–16, 65, 201
Commodity/commodities, 101, 132
  futures, 129
  prices, 4
  traders, 108, 140
  trading, 134
Commonality, 121
  see Edge, Trader
Competence, 197
Competition, 74, 91
  see Personal
Concentration, focus, 51, 63, 198
Conditioning, 15, 17
  see Behavioral
Confidence, 4, 8, 12, 17, 25, 29, 31, 34, 57, 72, 86, 116–18, 123, 124, 174, 197
  see Self-confidence
  level, 3
  psychology, 78
Consistency, 25, 28, 171, 173
  see Inconsistency, Methodology
Constructing, see Behavior
Continuation patterns, 183–85
Contract(s), 151, 182
  position, 141
Control
  see Personal, Risk, State of mind
  fear, 29
Conviction, 12, 15, 16, 81, 86, 101, 123, 174
Cootner, Paul, 129

D

Decision, 96, 113, 198
  see Market, Objective, Trading

Decision-making, 70, 108
  process, 110
Dedication, 130
Dennis, Richard, 143
Depressed/depression, 47, 98, 125, 153
Discipline, 4, 14, 17, 25, 31, 32, 78, 85, 96, 97, 109–111, 113, 116, 119, 123, 124, 130, 131, 134, 135, 155, 171, 173, 197, 201
Distribution, 179, 180
Downside
  breakout, 174
  definition, 9

E

Economics, 88–89
Edge(s), 134
  see Winning
  commonalities, 31-32
  definition, 33-34
  difference, 31-34
Efficient market theory, 161–67
Ego, 113, 114, 198
Elliott Wave, 11
Emotion(s), 93, 96, 130, 134, 135, 138, 139
  control, 25
Emotional barriers, 169
Empowering/empowerment, 16
  see Positive/empowering
Entry and/or exit, 158, 164–67
  markets, 71
Equity, 132, 134, 170
  see Margin-to-equity
  management, 169
  preservation, 172
Euphoric trading, 9, 10, 29, 96–97, 135, 191
Excellence, 198

see Avenue, External
modeling, 35–66
personal standard, establishment,
    196–97
standard, 195
Exhaustion gap, 186
Exit, 172
see Entry
Experience, 116, 123
Expertise, 32
External
  excellence, 41
  state of mind, 45
  strategy, 72

F

Failure, 41, 69, 126, 192
  see Personal
  fear, 28-29, 121-122
Fan(s), 176
Fast moving averages, 164–65
Faulkner, Elmer, 102–03
Fear, *see* Control, Failure, Inade-
    quacy, Losing, Success
Feeling(s), 47–48, 59-60, 71–72, 118,
    135, 137, 151, 153
Fibonnaci, 11
Fills, 27, 52, 70, 101
Flags, 183–84
Flexibility, 70, 130
Floor traders, 61
Focus, 3, 8, 70, 113, 116, 130, 134,
    136, 137, 139, 146, 172, 201
  see Attention, Concentration, Op-
      portunity, Poor, Positive/em-
      powering, Trading
  ability, 124
  comparison, *see* Losing/winning
  development, 111–12
  power, 19–20

Four Cs, *see* Trader
Friedman, Milton, 88
Fundamental
  analysis, 31
  approach, 102
  basis, 83
Fundamentalist, 133, 152, 159
Fundamentals, 82, 86, 103, 104, 130,
    133
Futures
  see Commodity
  industry, 4, 71, 188
  market, 3, 4, 6, 104, 159
  traders, 134
  trading, 169
    leverage, 73

G

Gann, 11
Gap(s), 185–88
  see Exhaustion, Measuring, Run-
      away
  patterns, 186
  types, 185–87
Goal(s), 4, 15, 32, 121, 197
  see Long-term, Objective, Personal,
      Psychological, Short-term,
      Trading
  achievement, 24, 26, 73
  prevention, 24
  strategy, 26
  concentration, 23
  establishment, 23, 200
  setting, 8, 21–29, 63
Greenberg, Joel, 5, 71, 73, 80, 86, 121,
    146–49, 152

H

Highs/lows, 164, 166

I

Ill-defined personal strategy, 26, 28
Imagery, 198
    see Audio, Kinesthetic, Mental, Visual
Inadequacy, fear, 29
Inconsistency, see Approach, Methodology
Independence, 128
Information, 90, 187
    see Market
Informational flows, 103
Innergame(s), 1–34
Internal
    communication, 199–200
    dialogue, see Successful
    processes, see State of mind
    state of mind, 41, 44–45
    strategy, 39, 72
    vocabulary usage, comparison, 61
Island reversal, 186

J

Johnson, Bruce, 71, 138, 145–155

K

Kamikaze trading, 9, 10
Key reversal, 182
Kinesthetic, 59-60, 71, 198
    imagery, 63
King, Marlow, 102, 103
Knowledge, 77
    see Outcome

L

Leverage, 132, 134, 140, 169
    see Futures

Life experience, 112, 113, 124, 126
Lifestyle, 128, 147
Limit bids, 78
Limited risk, 25
Limiting beliefs, 54–55
Liquid markets, 7
Logic, 95, 103
Long-term
    goal(s), 23, 24, 26
    motive, 32
    signal, 132, 133
    trader, 131, 133
Losers, 97, 98
    see Winners/losers
Losing, 32, 41, 56, 115, 116, 136
    fear, 123, 134
    strategies, 14
    trade, 80
    traders, characteristics, 70
Losing/winning
    comparison, 189–202
    traders, focus comparison, 51–52
Loss(es), 7, 81, 94, 97, 169, 171, 191
    see Profit and loss
    definition, 8, 9, 25, 191
    point, 136
    self-fulfilling prophecy, 52
    taking, 9
Lows, see Highs/lows

M

Management, see Equity, Money,
    Risk, State, Well-defined
Marden, Orison Swett, 192
Margin requirements, 131
Margin-to-equity ratio, 132
Market(s)
    see Breaking, Entry, Liquid, Moving, Universal
    action, 28, 39, 171

attraction, 89, 90
axioms, 69
behaviors, 8
beliefs, 71
conditions, 91
decisions, 72, 96
direction, 133
forecasting, 130
information, 56, 59
movement, 166
opportunity/opportunities, 170,
    174
pattern, 175
performance, 54
  prediction, 52
possibilities, 191
psychology, 174, 176
reaction, 101
rules, 69
signal, identification, 72
strength, 99
strength/weakness, 185
theory, *see* Efficient
value, 102
  opinion, 90
view, 51
Marketplace, 16, 104, 114, 129, 135,
    177
McVane, Charlie, 143
Measuring gap, 185
Melamed, Leo, 71, 73, 87–105, 123,
    192
Mental
  conditioning, 8
  imagery, 59
  outlook, 147
Merc, *see* Chicago
Methodology/methodologies, 28,
    31–32, 117, 122, 159, 169
  consistency, 69

inconsistency, 70
Midas touch, 3
Modeling behavior, 122
Monaster, Monty, 132
Money, ability to lose, 77
Money management, 79, 93, 131,
    134, 160, 169–70, 191
  program, 9, 12
Monterano, Tony, 145, 146
Motivation, 21-29, 69, 73-75
  see Personal
Motive, 4-6, 32, 73-75, 108, 197
  see Long-term, Psychological, Trad-
    ing
Moving averages, 161, 166 173–74
  see Fast
Moving market, 173

N

Negative attitude, 70
Negative/positive self-talk compari-
    son, 60–61
Nerve, 77
Numbers, hesitation, 9, 11

O

Objective
  decision, 173
  goals, 85
Obstacles, 196
October 1987 stock market crash, 42,
    150
Opportunity/opportunities, 77, 79,
    91, 108, 171, 174, 183, 196
  see Buying, Market
  focus, 9, 11, 25, 191
Orders, usage, 7
Outcome, 152, 196

knowledge, 13, 14
Overdiversification, 102
Overtrade/overtrading, 7, 85, 135

P

Patience, 31–32, 132
Performance, 46, 55, 57, 195
  see Market, Trader, Trading
  compensation, 128
Personal
  achievement, 42
  belief, 3, 6
    system, 4, 121
  competition, 91
  control, 61
  fulfillment, 201
  goals, 25
  failure, 192
  involvement, 184
  motivation, 8, 23
  responsibility, 29, 58, 69, 198
  strategy, 21, 33
    see Ill-defined
  trading state, 44–45
  trading system, understanding, 54–56
  training, 22
Personality, 92, 99, 104, 108
  profile, 124
  psychological characteristics, 92–93
Peters, Ralph, 100
Physical
  energy, lack, 26, 28
  scale, see Trading day
Physiology, 46, 48
  exercises, 49–50
Pit trader, 91, 100
Plan of action, see Action
Poor focus, 26, 27–28

Position(s), 80, 82, 95, 100, 130, 135, 139, 172, 180
  see Contract, Psychological
Positive
  attitude, 70, 149, 155
  beliefs, 16
  self-talk, 50, 58
    see Negative/positive
  state of mind, 34, 41, 43
Positive/empowering
  beliefs/focus, 33
  self-talk, 8
Price(s), 91, 110, 165, 174, 180, 191–92
  see Commodity
  action, 4
  levels, 159
  movement, 171
  structure, 99
Procedures, concentration, 23
Professional trader, 4
Profit(s), 7, 11, 111, 169, 174, 176, 183, 191, 193
  see Trading
  potential, 25
  taking, 9
Profit and loss, 96, 193
Psychological
  barriers, 12, 94, 113, 114, 130–31, 133, 134, 147–50, 169, 171–72, 187–88
    see Successful trader
  characteristics, see Personality
  energy, 26, 28
  factors, 8, 81
  goals, 63
  makeup, 92, 188
  motives, 63
  position, 42

pressure, 148, 155, 188
skills, 63, 66, 86, 160, 170, 184, 192–193
  see Successful trader
state of mind, 196
tolerances, 63
Psychology, 46, 92, 98, 104, 129
  see Behavrioral, Confidence, Market, Self-esteem, Trader
limits, 163

R

Rectangles, 183–84
Reevaluation/retooling, 13, 14
Resilience/resiliency, 70, 120
Resistance, 174, 175–77
Response, 70
Responsibility, 70
  see Personal
Retracement, 164, 167, 176–78, 185
Reversal, 101
  see Island, Key
day, 182
patterns, 180–82
Reward, *see* Risk/reward
Richey, Joe, 143
Risk, 93, 132, 172, 176
  see Limited
control, 32
management, 101
  see Well-defined
trade, 177
Risk/reward ratio, 32, 133
Risk-taker, 93
Robbins, Anthony, 46
Rockefeller, John D., 3
Role models, 99, 101, 122, 141, 142, 154–55
Rufenacht, Bob, 146, 155

Rules, 53–57, 95
  see Market, Trading, Winners/losers
Runaway gap, 185

S

Sandner, John F. (Jack), 71, 107–126
Segal, George, 10, 71, 79, 123, 146, 193
Self-confidence, 74, 78, 113, 123, 136, 198
Self-esteem, 3, 12, 25, 29, 33, 72, 118, 126, 201
psychology, 78
Self-fulfilling prophecy, 171
  see Losses
Self-limiting goals, 26, 27
Self-talk, 95
  see Negative/positive, Positive, Positive/empowering
Self-trust, 12
Self-worth, 28, 114
Shear, Sydney, 99, 100
Short-term
goals, 23
trader, 100, 133
Siegel, Joseph, 71, 74, 77, 85
Signals, 25, 95, 101, 131, 163, 173
  see Long-term
Silverman, Jeffrey L., 71, 127–143, 180
Simmons, Roy, 101
Skills, 108
  see Psychological
Smith, Adam, 88
Smoothing, 161
Spread, 137
values, 101
State management, 8

State(s) of mind, 3, 4, 9, 12, 33, 42-
    44, 70, 95, 117, 140, 188, 201
    see External, Internal, Positive, Psy-
        chological, Trading, Unresour-
        ceful, Winning
    control, 63
    enhancement, internal processes,
        59–60
    improvement, 58–59
Stevens, Donald, 71, 78
Stock market crash, see October
Strategy/strategies, 4, 32, 38, 174
    see External, Goal, Ill-defined, Inter-
        nal, Losing, Personal, Techni-
        cal, Trading, Winning
Strengths/weaknesses, 63–66
    see Market
Success, 41, 170, 197, 201
    see Trading
    fear, 29
    formula, 72
    internal atmosphere, 195
    internal environment, creation,
        197–98
Successful internal dialogue, crea-
    tion formula, 198–99
Successful trader, 4, 6, 38, 52, 57, 71,
    92, 104, 108, 110, 113, 114, 124,
    129, 142, 146
    nature, 13–17
    psychological barriers, 9–12
    psychological skills, 8
    psychological traits, 129–30
Successful trading, 6, 44, 71, 77–83,
    94, 147, 200, 202
    characteristics, 13-14
    principles, 191–94
    syntax, 37-39
Supply and demand, 74, 81, 88, 90,
    91, 102, 103

factors, 82
Support, 174–77
System
    application, see Trading
    development, 25

T

Technical(s), 102–103
Technical
    analysis, 31, 186
        psychology, 157–188
    approach, 102
    interpretation, 104
    strategies, 189
Technicians, 86, 103, 133, 159
Techniques, 4
Tenacity, 81
Time frame, 159
Tolerances
    see Psychological
    levels, 91
Top traders, 41, 46, 50, 61, 67–155,
    188, 191
    innergame, 72
Top(s), 180–82
Trade(s)
    see Losing, Risk, Winning
    control, 25
    reasons, 4–6
Trader(s)
    see Commodity, Floor, Futures,
        Long-term, Losing, Pit, Profes-
        sional, Short-term, Successful,
        Top, Winning
    commonality, 14–15
    Four Cs, 15–17
    innergame, 72
    performance, 58
    psychology, 91, 180
    strengths/weaknesses, 64

Trading
  see Commodity, Euphoric, Futures,
      Kamikaze, Successful
  actions, 6
  anxiety, sources, 28-29
  axioms, 7, 9
  behavior, manifestations, 28-29
  capital, 78
  day, 97
    physical scale, 50
  decisions, 199
  enjoyment, 65
  experiences, 149
  focus, 51
  goals, 22–23, 46, 197
    factor barriers, 26–28
    operational definition, 23–26
  interest, 64
  love, 31
  motive, 200
    understanding, 33
  performance, 66
  process, 20, 32, 143
  profit, 62
  rules, 7, 57
  state(s) of mind, 45, 60
    see Personal
  strategy, 6, 66
  style, 6, 130
    personality matching, 63–66
  success, 169
  system, 63, 66, 159, 160, 173–74, 188
    see Personal
    application, 9, 11
Trend(s), 161–167, 174
  see Uptrend
  definition, 159
  identification, 161–63
  identifiers, 161–64
  phases, 179–80

Trendline(s), 161, 166, 171, 173, 176,
    183
Triangles, 183–84
Trust, 33, 199

U

Universal beliefs, 52
  markets, 52-53
Unresourceful state of mind, 26, 27
Uptrend, 165, 171
  line, 173

V

Value, 91
  see Market, Spread
Van Hess, 77, 78
Visual, 71, 198
  imagery, 63
Volatility, 180

W

Weaknesses, *see* Strengths/weak-
    nesses
Well-defined risk management, 32
Winners, 86, 93, 97, 98, 114
Winners/losers
  belief system comparison, 56
  rules comparison, 57
Winning
  characteristics, 195-202
  definition, 113
  edge, 201
  losing comparison, *see* Losing/win-
    ning
  results, 187
  states of mind, 41–62
    exercises, 44–45, 49-50, 54–56, 57–
      58, 60

psychological characteristics, 195
  syntax, 42
strategies, 14
trade(s), 12, 57, 79
traders, 93
  characteristics, 69–70

focus comparison, *see* Losing/winning
Wycoff, 11

Z

Ziglar, Zig, 200

ABOUT THE AUTHORS

Robert Koppel is a former member of the Chicago Mercantile Exchange. He is currently Director of Trading at Abell Asset Management Corp. He is a frequent seminar speaker who lectures on the internal elements of successful trading. He holds advanced degrees in Philosophy and Group Behavior from Columbia University.

Howard Abell is President of Abell Asset Management Corp., a CTA firm managing individual and institutional portfolios. A former member of the Chicago Board of Trade and the Chicago Mercantile Exchange, he was President of C.S.A. Inc., a Futures Commission Merchant. He is the co-author of *The Insider's Edge* (Probus, 1985).